I BET YOU

I Bet You

A history of the members of
the Berwick Salmon Club
from 1841 to 2000
and the interesting wagers
they laid after dinner

Eric Grounds

Published on Lulu 2012

by Eric Grounds
Shellacres Farm
Cornhill on Tweed
Northumberland TD12 4XB

© Eric Grounds 2012

The moral right of the author has been asserted

ISBN 978-1-4717-3283-6

Book design and cover by
Curran Publishing Services Ltd
Norwich, UK

Contents

Introduction

The wise reader will not try to read this book from front to back. The best plan is to pick it up, open any page and enjoy a snatched view of history through the eyes of men who have enjoyed a good dinner. The stories unfold pretty much in chronological order, although there are three collated summaries of information on farming, fishing and Oxbridge competitions towards the back of the book.

Every attempt has been made to validate the information about people and events. Google, Wikipedia and other online search resources have made the task much easier but they are not necessarily wholly accurate. I have not always accepted them at face value but admit that I have not amended a great deal of information drawn from their records. Where there is an important source that should be mentioned, the information is properly recorded by the relevant item. I take this opportunity to acknowledge the excellence and scholarship of those who have contributed to the anthology of information.

There will be mistakes, and I take full responsibility for any lack of perfection.

I do need to thank many people for their help and encouragement. The members of the Salmon Club have been kind, thoughtful and supportive throughout, and I owe a particular debt to Rob Dick and Andrew Douglas Home, who have both gone the extra mile to help me improve the product. I would like to thank Linda Bankier, the borough archivist, for her professional knowledge and absolute determination to point me towards success. I am hugely grateful to Ian Martin, the Archivist at the King's Own Scottish Borderers Museum in Berwick, who helped me to put a great deal of flesh on the biographies of KOSB members of the Berwick Salmon Club and who revealed the existence of the Club's missing photograph album. It is entirely thanks to Ian that we have been able to publish pictures of the earliest members in this history. Both Jim Coats and John Rae, respected elders of their own Berwick dining clubs, have been uniformly kind and helpful, while Chris Leyland and John Home Robertson added humour and helpful insights to problems that puzzled me during the project. Jim Taylor and Tom Fairfax most generously took me to dine with their clubs, thereby illuminating my interest in the many and varied practices of Britain's bons viveurs. And I must not forget to thank Joe Green, whose scholarship and literary knowledge stunned me with unexpected information about Anthony Trollope, which added to the story of the Titchborne claimant.

I am unable to name all of those kind-hearted friends and associates who have had to put up with me telling them about the book and its contents, but I do thank them most sincerely for their patience and support.

The book has been improved immensely by the generosity of John Burnett, who agreed to allow us to publish sketches and caricatures of club members drawn by his late father, Sir David Burnett, Bt., who was a member of the club from 1979 to 1997. Sir David was a prolific artist whose subjects rarely knew that he had drawn them. His entire collection, seen by very few people outside the Burnett family, is a monument to a lifetime interest.

Finally, thanks are due to Susan Curran, who edited and typeset the book, and to Antony Chessell, who steered me towards Lulu and took exceptional trouble to show me what to do.

1
The establishment of dining clubs

The late eighteenth century saw the formation of the earliest 'gentlemen's clubs', which were created to provide a discreet environment for members, who were generally aristocratic, to pursue their interest in gambling or political debate. The clubs replaced the role of coffee houses which had been established earlier in the century, largely because the members desired more privacy.

By the end of the 1800s, there were more than 400 clubs in London alone. The oldest remaining club is White's, which was founded in 1693. But other cities played their part, with Liverpool's Athenaeum Club established in 1797 by art collector and social reformer, William Roscoe, and the Clifton Club in Bristol founded in 1818. The Select Society of Auctioneers established their dining club in 1795 and continue to enjoy three dinners each year at Boodles.

Rural communities had less need for their own bricks and mortar, so a range of dining clubs evolved, each with their own distinctive practices and culture. Recorders, which has up to 38 members from Northumberland, Tyne & Wear and Co. Durham, was founded in 1747, while the Tweeddale Shooting Club, established in 1766, still meets two to three times a year at the Tontine Hotel in Peebles, where they actually own the freehold of the dining room and cellar. The members wear white tie and an elegant green tail coat. They allow no speeches, do not lay wagers, but may take a guest. The Forest Club was founded in 1788 and the Jedforest was established by the earl of Ancrum in 1810. The Jedforest celebrated its anniversary in 2010 at Monteviot, inviting members' wives for the first time in 200 years.

Berwick-upon-Tweed boasts three dining clubs. Established in 1743, the oldest Berwick club is fortunate to have artefacts which serve as tangible tokens of the club's antiquity. But sadly most of the paper records were lost in a fire when Mr Hamish Edgar was the club secretary. Its style is substantially different from the two younger clubs. With 40 members, it meets twice a year (once for the AGM, and once for dinner, normally on

15 February). Club members are expected to entertain their colleagues, so there are songs, recitations, stories and readings. They always start their dinner with the Berwick Salmon song and they often sing choral works between courses.

The youngest of the Berwick clubs, the Tweed Salmon Dinner Club, was established in 1854, and thanks to John Reay, who became its secretary in 1971, it has published a brief history for the period 1854–1989 and a supplement, which covers 1989–2009.

2
Origins of the Berwick Salmon Club, founded 1841

The Berwick Salmon Club, which is the subject of this book, has two meetings annually. On the first occasion, normally in October or November, the members discuss the dinner which is to be held the following February. Members drink, normally champagne, at the expense of the club. Attendance has been inconsistent over the years, and from time to time the secretary of the day has barked at his colleagues in order to persuade them to play an active part in their affairs. But attendance at the dinner is normally excellent, not least because every member must pay even if they fail to attend.

On Tuesday 15 February 1842, eleven members enjoyed dinner for the princely sum of £8 11s 8d. The purchasing power of an 1840 £1 sterling was £42.39 in 2009, so in today's terms, the dinner cost £363.71, or £33 per head. The cost per head of the 2009 dinner was £98. The higher cost per head may be attributed mainly to the higher quality of wines which the members enjoy drinking.

There are two aspects of the club which make it interesting: its members, and the wagers that they lay after dinner. This history seeks to weave both into a single narrative showing some of the social and cultural interests of the day. It strives to adopt a broad view of the social life of the Borders and the wider world in the nineteenth and twentieth centuries.

Someone has said that the club was established in 1834, but with no artefacts or written records to support it, we have to accept that 1841 is the start point. The first recorded meeting took place in the Hen and Chickens Inn, Berwick-upon-Tweed, in the late afternoon of 15 February 1841. Those attending were:

Mr Thomas Cockburn in the chair
Mr John Dewar
Mr George Henderson
Mr Thomas Hubback
Mr Alexander Lowrey

Mr George Marshall
Mr Kenneth McKenzie
Mr George Paterson
Mr George Sanderson
Mr Andrew Scott
Mr Henry Short
Mr James Weddell
and Dr Samuel Edgar, who joined the party after dinner.

There is no clear relationship between the members, other than that three were guardians of the Poor Law Union at the time (Messrs Dewar, Hubback and Lowrey). The link with the Poor Law Union stretched somewhat further because later members of the club also served: Mr Charles Gilchrist (a member of the club from 1848–1878), Mr Alexander Kirkwood (1847–1865), Mr James Marshall (1848–1860), and Mr Edward Willoby (1850–1882).

Mr Willoby was clerk to the guardians of the Poor Law Union from its formation in 1836. He served for a substantial fifty-two years, at first in partnership with his father, William, with whom he practised in the firm of W&E Willoby, then continuing alone after his father's death in 1856. The death of William was unusual: he was alone in his sitting room reading up on a forthcoming case in the court. Somehow his clothing caught fire from a candle and by the time his cries were heard by his son Edward, he was very seriously burned. He died two days later.

The family could

Edward Willoby Sr, member 1850–82

claim a public connection with Berwick for more than two centuries, with all the men of the family being admitted as freemen. His father and grandfather both served as town clerk, and the family lived at 32–36 Ravensdowne.

Mr Willoby had two sons and two daughters. The elder son, William, became a lawyer and duly joined the family firm which became E&W Willoby. But in 1885 William died at the early age of 45. Edward, the younger son, had become a land agent, so Edward senior found an external partner, Henry Alder Peters (a member of the Salmon Club from 1882 to 1907) which produced a third change of business name to Willoby & Peters. Mr Peters became clerk to the Board of Guardians of the Poor Law when Mr Edward Willoby resigned in 1888.

Of the twelve original diners, two (Mr McKenzie and Mr Paterson) were never seen again. Mr George Sanderson turned out for the 1842 dinner but then disappeared. Messrs Short, Scott and Dewar attended for four, five and seven years respectively. But Mr Hubback was a member for thirty-two years, Mr Weddell for forty-two years and Mr Lowrey for forty-nine years, this being a record beaten only by the late Mr Allan Herriot, who was a member from 1948 to 1999 and who missed only three dinners in fifty-two years (1988, 1990 and 1991).

Dr Samuel Edgar is interesting for a different reason. In 1849 he failed to attend the dinner, despite having intimated that he would be present. Those who were present at that dinner instantly voted that he should no longer be a member of the club. He became the founder chairman of the Tweed Salmon Dinner Club in 1854 but resigned in 1858. He was alderman of Berwick in 1855. One or two other members of the three clubs seem to have flowed from one to another, including Mr Thomas Allan, a founder member of the Tweed Salmon Dinner Club, who dined with them from 1854 to 1868, then joined the Berwick Salmon Club in 1871 and remained until 1884. Mr Allan was a timber and slate merchant in a business which became Allan Brothers. Born in 1825, he served as sheriff of Berwick in 1859 and 1869 and was mayor in 1861. He died in 1892.

The choice of date for dinner for all three Berwick dining clubs paid tribute to the opening of the net fishing season, which was traditionally on 14 February.

The club normally dined at the Kings Arms Hotel, although it used the Red Lion ten times between 1847 and 1861, and the Salmon Inn in 1854, 1862 and 1863. But after almost 120 years of loyalty, the secretary reported to the business meeting on 28 January 1961 that:

The Manager of the Kings Arms Hotel had told him that it was most inconvenient for the Club to have the exclusive use of the Dining Room for its annual dinner from about 6.30pm to after midnight and that he offered the Club the use of the small sitting room in which this meeting was being held (the upstairs cocktail bar attached to the Assembly Rooms having been booked for another function). If that was not acceptable, he would be prepared to allow us the main Dining Room. After a lengthy discussion, in which it was agreed that the Smoke Room was much too small and it was suggested that the use of the Dining Room was obviously being offered to us on sufferance, it was pointed out that there was no private car park attached to the Kings Arms, it was resolved that Tillmouth Park Hotel be approached and if they were willing to accommodate us with a suitable private room and could give us the sort of meal and wines we required, the Dinner this year should be held at that Hotel.

The club never returned to the Kings Arms, and the dinner on 15 February 1961 took place in the Tillmouth Park Hotel, which hosted the club until 1966. There was some turbulence in the following years. The Collingwood Arms in Cornhill became the venue until 1969, when the club moved to the Castle Hotel in Berwick. There was a return to Tillmouth Park from 1970 to 1973. The Turret House Hotel hosted dinner in 1974 and 1975, but the 1976 dinner was held in the KOSB Officers Mess, thanks to Lt Col Philip Harrison, who was the regimental secretary. Many of the former military members of the club enjoyed happy hours drinking gin with Philip in his mess over the years, with Lt Col Pat de Clermont and Lt Col Johnny Collingwood attending so often that they became honorary members of the mess (thereby being able to maintain their own mess bills). The Turret House Hotel was the venue again in 1977, and was used annually until 1985, when the club returned to the Tillmouth Park Hotel once more.

Tillmouth Park lost favour as the result of an idiotic error by the chef in 1987. During his meeting with the secretary to confirm the menu, he failed to understand what was meant by the term 'salmon in its brine' (pronounced 'breen'). Come the evening of the dinner, the diners were considerably surprised to receive poached salmon with a lump of cold pasteurised brie on top. The members were mildly rattled, so leaped at the chance offered by the arrival of a gifted chef at Western House, Lowick in 1987. He certainly provided a good dinner on 17 April 1988 but he did not stay in the area for more than fifteen months, so dinner was held at the Wheatsheaf Hotel, Swinton from 1989 to 1992.

The business meeting of the club in 1992 had the lowest turnout of members in years. This created a huge amount of additional work for the poor secretary (Mr Robert Dick), because he had to canvass opinion from individuals about a suitable venue, since no hotel seemed to be able to provide what the members sought. It was by default, therefore, that dinner was held at the Castle Hotel, Greenlaw on 15 April 1993. Sadly it was not a roaring success, although the bill for the evening was only £45 per head. The meal was perfectly acceptable but in no way special, and with only eleven members present, the occasion felt a little flat.

Having made a point with Tillmouth Park, both sides were content for the club to return in 1994, and for a dozen years the annual dinner was enjoyed in a large private room, normally supervised by Ms Shirley Lauder, whose team worked hard at making the event enjoyable.

But the members realised a growing disillusion with hotels, not least because of the smoking laws which came into force on 1 July 2007. At the AGM on 10 November 2008 members were asked to volunteer to host the dinner. Mr George Farr of Pallinsburn swiftly put his wonderful house at the disposal of the club, and a most successful and delicious dinner was held there on Monday 16 February 2009. Mrs Fiona Burn, who ran a local catering business, did the cooking and deployed her team of waitresses to serve. This was an important strand to the thinking of the members, who did not want to impose upon their hostess by asking her to cook. And, if the truth is to be told, no one could contemplate the idea of complaining if the meal fell below the very demanding standards the members desired.

3
The early years, 1841–1889

The selection of this time frame is based on the membership of the longest-serving founder member, Mr Alexander Lowrey, who was a farmer at Castle Hills and died in 1889. His first wager was not laid until 15 February 1844, when he bet Mr Andrew Scott three bottles of wine that the average price of corn during the year ending 31 December 1844 would be better than that ending 31 December 1843. The average was to be taken from the corn inspector's returns. We do not know what the price was, but Mr Scott lost.

Alexander Lowrey, member 1841–89

His final wager in 1889 was with Mr Robert Bolam, that Champion potatoes would not be 35/- per ton on the first Saturday in February 1890. Mr Bolam lost because the average price was 30/-. Sadly Mr Lowrey never knew the result because he died shortly before the 1890 dinner.

Unlike the modern-day club, roughly half of the members in the 1840s were bachelors, so a regular wager was that one or more would be wed before the next dinner. Two of the six bachelors attending the 1841 dinner, Mr Thomas Hubback and Mr Henry Short, were indeed married before the following year.

Mr Hubback, who was a member of the club from 1841 to 1872, was a guardian of the Berwick-upon-Tweed Poor Law Union and appears to have been in business with one John Gray. In 1855 the *London Gazette* published the information that:

> the Partnership formerly subsisting between us the undersigned, Thomas Hubback and John Gray, as Clothiers and Hatters, in Berwick-upon-Tweed, was on the 31st day of December, 1853, dissolved by mutual consent.—Dated this 20th day of January, 1855.

Mr Hubback offers a helpful snapshot of contemporary thoughts. He wagered in 1848 'that the Bridge across the Tweed will be opened for railway traffic on or before the 1st day of August 1848.' In fact the Royal Border Bridge, which is a Grade 1 listed railway viaduct, was opened by Queen Victoria in 1850. The engineer who designed it was Robert Stephenson (son of George Stephenson).

Over the next two years, Mr Hubback stuck with his railway theme, twice betting that the Kelso branches of the York Newcastle & Berwick and the North British Railways would be joined for general traffic. He lost on both occasions, so turned his attention to statistics on wheat production and fishing.

On 15 February 1855 Dr Kirkwood laid a wager with Mr Hubback that the price of Peruvian guano would be as high in twelve months as it was that day. At £12 per ton, it was seen to be an expensive product. Guano manure was an effective fertiliser and gunpowder ingredient due to its high levels of phosphorus and nitrogen. Its lack of odour was an advantage. In 1857 Mr Hubback predicted that the price would be 40/- lower in 1858, and lost.

Mr Hubback slowly withdrew from the club and finally resigned in 1865, although he was exhorted to remain an honorary member and encouraged to attend the dinner when it suited him. Perhaps the last interesting wager in which he was involved was on 15 February 1861, when Mr Lowrey bet Mr Bogue that there would be no prosecution for bribery arising out of the Report of the Commissioners regarding the Berwick Election Enquiry by 5 February 1862. Mr Willoby promptly bet Mr Hubback that there would not be any conviction arising out of the same enquiry by the same date.

The wager was lost by Mr Hubback. As background, the UK House of

Commons Journals for 24 January 1860 show that the attorney general was directed to prosecute William McGall for giving perjured evidence to the Committee of Elections investigating the Berwick-Upon-Tweed election.

The seat had sent members to Parliament since its enfranchisement by Henry VIII. Initially it sent two members although this was reduced to one in 1885. The Conservative Ralph Anstruther Earle (1835–10 June 1879) was elected at the May 1859 general election but resigned from the House of Commons within weeks. Dudley Marjoribanks, a Liberal who had been one of the members from 1853 until the May 1859 election, was re-elected in his place the following August.

Mr Thomas Cockburn was the chairman for the first recorded dinner. A wine and spirit merchant, he regularly attended the Berwick Salmon Club dinners between 1841 and 1861, but was not a major participant in the laying of wagers, initiating twenty-one and accepting just ten in his first twenty years of membership. But in 1860, 1861, 1862 and 1863, when he was not in attendance, two wagers were laid in his name and three were accepted; he lost all but one. This convention continues, and from time to time unsuspecting members who fail to attend the dinner discover after the event that they have had to accept unwinnable wagers. It is worth mentioning that convention demands that a member must accept a wager, however ridiculous, although he may barter about the precise terms.

The vast majority of wagers are repeated year after year: the price of wheat and barley; the outcome of cricket, football and rugby internationals; the results of Oxford and Cambridge sporting meetings; and the number or size of fish caught in the River Tweed. Some of the information is interesting because of comparisons with modern times, so at the end of the book there are consolidated summaries of standard wagers from 1841 to 2010. Many wagers focused on political affairs – which party would be in power, who would be prime minister, and in more recent times, whether certain dictators in foreign lands would survive.

From time to time, individuals would be mentioned in wagers. In 1847, for example, Mr Dewar bet Mr Mallock one bottle of wine that the North British Railway would not be bought by or let to Mr Hudson before this day twelvemonth. Mr Mallock lost. But who was Mr Hudson?

The mid-1840s saw George Hudson at his most powerful, with influential friends in both politics and business. Even the prime minister, the Duke of Wellington, was said to be grateful to him, and George Stephenson joined him in business ventures for a while, until he became wary. W. E. Gladstone spoke positively about him after his death, although pro-Hudson supporters in the House of Commons often thwarted

Gladstone's attempts to bring in national control of the railways. By 1844 he controlled more than 1,000 miles of railway (about 30 per cent of the whole British railway system) and was dubbed the Railway King. His wealth allowed him to buy several Yorkshire estates, including the 12,000-acre Londesborough estate and Newby Park.

Hudson spent £80,000 opposing the Railway Bill. He also bought the Eastern Counties line, which proved to be unwise. This action contributed to his ultimate failure. By the end of 1847 share prices began to decline. Hudson had to resign from all the companies of which he was a director. Many of the shareholders were facing ruin. By clever political manipulation Hudson had avoided government regulation of the railway business, but a committee of investigation managed to expose many of the scandals that his business dealings had created. Hudson agreed to pay back the shareholders of the Great North Railway and the Newcastle and Berwick Railway because he had defrauded them in business.

Hudson fled his creditors and went to live in France. He failed to pay his debts and ended up from July 1865 to October 1866 in York Castle, imprisoned as a debtor. Friends raised the money to get him out, after which he lived quietly in retirement in London thanks to the benevolence of his supporters. He died on 14 December 1871, and was buried near his birthplace at Scrayingham, York.

It was not until the dinner on 17 February 1851 that a new strand of thinking appeared. Mr George Henderson bet Mr William Paulin one bottle of wine that the electric telegraph would be in operation between England and France by the last account known from the newspaper by the club's next meeting.

Mr Henderson lost. It must be said that he had been quite optimistic, because the British Electric Telegraph Company was only incorporated by Special Act of Parliament on 29 July 1850, with a capital of £100,000 in 4,000 shares of £25. The company remained inert for two years, with no cable laid at all. But from 1853 growth was rapid, and by June 1854 it had seventy-one telegraph stations. Paris and London were linked in the autumn of that year.

On 15 February 1853, Dr Alexander Kirkwood bet Mr James Weddell one bottle of wine that the Jews would be legally admissible to Parliament by this time twelvemonths.

Dr Kirkwood lost. The issue was energetically contested between the Commons and the Lords for a number of years, even though Benjamin Disraeli, born a Jew though baptised into the Church of England at the age of twelve, was a member of Parliament from 1837. He served as chancellor of the Exchequer in the 1858 and 1867–1868 Conservative governments and went on to become prime minister in 1868 and again in 1874. He was elevated to the House of Lords in 1876. His willingness to take Christian oaths meant there were no barriers to his political career. For other Jews, the oath remained the key obstacle.

A Jewish candidate, Lionel de Rothschild, was elected as one of the four members of Parliament for the City of London in 1847, but was denied his seat because he would not take the Christian oath. He resigned, determined to test the will of the electorate. In 1849 he won a crushing majority, but was again unable to take his seat. Indeed, he was elected on no less than five occasions between 1847 and 1857 but was constantly denied the right to sit. Finally on Monday 26 July 1858 he took the oath with covered head, substituting 'so help me, Jehovah' for the ordinary form of oath, and thereupon took his seat as the first practising Jewish member of Parliament.

In 1850 David Salomons was elected to represent Greenwich and insisted upon taking his seat. The prime minister, Lord John Russell, demanded that he be ejected from the House, and, although the members responded with some sympathy to a compelling speech by Salomons, he was ordered by the speaker to withdraw. Salomons revealed his mettle by being elected lord mayor of London in 1855. By the time he was re-elected for Greenwich in a by-election in early 1859, Rothschild's success has created a precedent and he was able to take his seat. Two years later a more general form of oath for all members of Parliament was introduced, which freed the Jews from all cause for exclusion.

For the record Mr Weddell, who won the wager, was a founder member of the club, and his son and grandson followed in his wake, maintaining the family tradition of membership until Mr Arthur Weddell (secretary 1909–1921) resigned in 1921.

After dinner on 15 February 1855, Mr Thomas Hubback bet Mr Alexander Lowrey that there would be peace with Russia by this time twelvemonth.

Hubback lost because the peace which was confirmed by the Treaty of Paris was not signed until 30 March 1856. But herein lies the root of the misplaced tradition that Berwick-upon-Tweed is still at war with Russia.

Berwick changed hands between England and Scotland several times, and was traditionally regarded as a special, separate entity. Some proclamations referred to 'England, Scotland and the town of Berwick-upon-Tweed'. Many believe that one such was the declaration of the Crimean War against Russia in 1853, which Queen Victoria supposedly signed as 'Victoria, Queen of Great Britain, Ireland, Berwick-upon-

A family tradition: left above, James Weddell, member 1841–82; right above, Robert Weddell, member 1869–1908; left below, Arthur Weddell. member 1906–20

Tweed and all British Dominions'. However, when the Treaty of Paris (1856) was signed to conclude the war, Berwick-upon-Tweed was not mentioned. This meant that, supposedly, one of Britain's smallest towns was officially at war with one of the world's largest powers – and the conflict was extended by the lack of a peace treaty for over a century.

The BBC programme *Nationwide* investigated this story in the 1970s, and found that while Berwick was not mentioned in the Treaty of Paris, it was not mentioned in the declaration of war either. The question remained as to whether Berwick had ever been at war with Russia in the first place. The true situation is that since the Wales and Berwick Act 1746 had already made it clear that all references to England included Berwick, the town had no special status at either the start or end of the war.

Charles Gilchrist, a grocer and guardian of the Poor Law Union, became mayor of Berwick in 1869. On 15 February 1855 he bet Mr Edward Willoby that Sebastopol would be taken by the Allies by 15 May 1855.

Mr Gilchrist lost: Sebastopol fell in September 1855. The cascabels (the large balls at the rear of old muzzle-loaded guns) of several Russian cannons captured during the siege are still used to make the Victoria Cross, the highest award for gallantry in the British Armed Forces.

Occasionally the same wager was laid by different parties at the same dinner. In February 1857, Mr George Henderson bet Mr William Paulin and Mr George Marshall bet Mr James Marshall that the Queen's next baby would be a prince.

Mr Henderson and Mr George Marshall lost because the baby, born on 14 April 1857, was Princess Beatrice, who in 1885 married Prince Henry of Battenberg (1858–1896). Mr George Marshall did not attend the dinner, and the bet was made in his name by Mr Gilchrist, who signed the wager in company with Mr James Marshall. Poor Mr George Marshall died later in the year.

Royal babies regularly serve as the subject of a wager. At the Red Lion Hotel on 1 March 1858 Mr Thomas Bogue, who had the distinction of serving as mayor of Berwick four times (1852, 1858, 1859 and 1864), and who died on 5 December 1870, bet Mr John Meggison that Princess Frederick William of Prussia would give birth to a living child before 20 February 1859.

Mr Meggison lost. A son was born on 27 January 1859. Prince Frederick William Victor Albert of Prussia (often dubbed Kaiser Willie), who died on 4 June 1941, was the last German emperor and king of Prussia, ruling both the German Empire and the Kingdom of Prussia from 15 June 1888 to 9 November 1918.

A few years later in 1863 Mr Charles Gilchrist bet Mr Alexander Kirkwood that there would be a child born to the prince of Wales and his intended bride (Princess Alexandra of Denmark) within ten months after their marriage, which was to take place on 10 March. The princess gave birth to a son on 8 January 1864, so Mr Kirkwood lost. Then in 1865 Mr Thomas Bogue bet Mr Gilchrist that the princess of Wales would give birth to another child by 5 February 1866. Mr Gilchrist lost: a prince was born on 3 June 1865, and christened George Frederick Ernest Albert.

Local affairs produced some interesting material during this period. At the dinner in March 1858 Mr Edward Willoby bet Mr James Weddell that Mr James Stapleton, MP for Berwick, would be unseated before 20 February 1859 in consequence of his recent conviction. Mr Willoby lost, although Stapleton did lose his seat in an election in 1859; he was re-elected in 1868. Stapleton was one of the directors of the British Bank together with Humphrey Brown, Edward Esdaile, H. D. Macleod, Alderman R. H. Kennedy, W. D. Owen and Hugh Innes Cameron, who were convicted for fraud after a trial which lasted from 13 to 27 February 1858.

One year later, on 1 March 1859, Dr Alexander Kirkwood bet Mr Thomas Bogue that the New Wallace's Green Chapel would not be opened for public worship by the first Sunday in June 1859. Dr Kirkwood won the bet because the chapel opened on 19 June 1859.

That same night Mr George Henderson bet Mr Thomas Hubback one bottle of wine that Andrew Barclay, then committed for trial for an assault, would not be sentenced to more than three months imprisonment. Sadly the records of Barclay and his trial have been lost in the mists of time, but we do know that Mr Henderson lost.

At the Red Lion Hotel on 15 February 1860 Mr George Marshall, who attended seventeen dinners between 1841 and 1857, successfully bet Dr Kirkwood that the Berwick Volunteer Artillery Corps would not fire a piece of ordnance on exercise by 10 February 1861. A year later, Mr Thomas Hubback bet Mr Stephen Sanderson that not one of the Volunteer Artillery Corps of Berwick would hit the target in ordinary practice by 5 February 1862. Sanderson lost.

The evidence that the Volunteers did not do too well is an hilarious, if rather sobering reminder of the challenges facing the modern-day Territorial and Regular Army, which often finds itself prevented from realistic training because of the nation's financial condition.

On a wilder note Mr Thomas Johnson, attending his first dinner, bet Mr John Meggison, a former sheriff of Berwick, that the pope would be obliged to vacate Rome by 5 February 1863. Mr Johnson lost his bet, but we can see something of his reasoning in another wager laid that night when Dr Kirkwood bet one of four new members, Captain Smith RN, that the emperor of the French would have withdrawn his troops from Rome by 5 February 1863. This bet was lost by Dr Kirkwood, and Captain Smith, who lived at Ava Lodge, never returned for another dinner. Sadly we don't even know his Christian name.

War was a major issue in the 1860s. Captain Smith bet Mr Logan – it is not known if this was Mr William or Mr Ross Logan – in 1862 that if the war between North and South in the United States lasted till 1 January 1863, there would be no successful interference on the part of England or France to open ports. Mr Logan lost the wager.

Mr Thomas Hubback then bet Captain Smith that the ports of New Orleans and the Mississippi up to the Ohio would be opened by 1 August 1862. Mr Hubback lost. The debate continued in 1865, when Mr James Weddell bet Dr Henry Richardson that peace would not be re-established between the Northern and Southern States of America by the last known account before Christmas 1865. Mr Weddell lost because the American Civil War finally drew to an end.

Financial matters have been a consistent theme, and it is interesting today to see how taxation fluctuated from year to year. For example, Mr Thomas Bogue bet Mr Edward Willoby that income tax would be lower on 5 February 1866 than it was on 5 February 1865 (when it was 6 per cent). Mr Willoby lost because it dropped to fourpence in the pound (1.67 per cent). At the same time Mr John Meggison bet Mr Bogue that on 5 February 1866 the Bank of England's rate of interest would be higher than 5 per cent. He was right: it rose to 8 per cent.

On 17 February 1868 Mr Charles Gilchrist bet Mr George Smith (who attended only this one dinner, because he died before the dinner in 1869) that the Abyssinian Expedition would be terminated by 5 February 1869. The wager was lost by Mr Smith.

The British 1868 expedition to Abyssinia was a punitive mission carried out under the command of Lt.-Gen. Sir Robert Napier of the Bombay Army against the Ethiopian Empire, aimed at securing the release of European hostages. The force included 13,000 British and Indian soldiers, 26,000 camp followers and 40,000 animals. The decisive battle took place outside Magdala and was almost an anticlimax. The British repelled a massive attack, then routed the defending forces in just two hours the following day. The British casualties were two killed and eighteen wounded, while the Ethiopians lost 700 killed and 1,400 wounded.

Over the next two days Tewodros, the emperor, released the hostages, then committed suicide rather than be captured. Napier received a hereditary peerage and eventually advanced in rank to become a field marshal in 1883. He was installed as constable of the Tower of London in January 1887 and died in January 1890. He is buried in St Paul's Cathedral.

The Maynooth Grant exercised Mr Thomas Johnson, a member from 1862–1885, who bet Mr Joseph Ruddock in 1869 and 1870 that the grant would be abolished by 5 February the following year. Mr Johnson lost on both occasions.

It is surprising that this wager was laid as late as 1869, because the Maynooth Grant was a major British political controversy back in the 1840s. In 1845 the prime minister, Sir Robert Peel, sought to put a stop to political unrest in Ireland. One of his conciliatory proposals was that the Royal College of St Patrick, a Catholic seminary at Maynooth, should have its annual grant increased from £9,000 (a figure that had remained constant since 1809) to £26,000. In a one-time payment, the seminary would receive an additional £30,000 for repairs. The seminary had been receiving a grant since it had been founded by King George III in 1795 as a way of avoiding having priests trained in revolutionary France. Peel felt that a better-educated clergy would be less likely to support causes such as the repeal of the Act of Union.

While the grant was controversial, and weakened Peel's government, it set a precedent, and within three years, government support was being given to Catholic schools in England.

1869 was a good year for Catholic intrigue and debate. Mr Edward Willoby bet Mr Thomas Johnson that in the case *Saurin* v. *Starr & Others* the verdict would be in favour of the defendant. The wager was lost by Mr Willoby.

The plaintiff, Sister Mary Saurin, who won substantial damages, was a nun. She had brought an action for conspiracy and false imprisonment against the mother superior of a convent of Sisters of Mercy at Hull, at whose hands she alleged that she had suffered many grievances. The trial went into elaborate detail about the miserable life of nuns at the time, with claim and counter-claims being made on both sides. John Coleridge acted for Sister Saurin, and the trial was almost unprecedented in its duration. Coleridge went on to become the lord chief justice in 1880.

Although there is a consolidated summary of fishing wagers later in this book, eager fishermen will be interested to learn that at the 1869 dinner Mr Thomas Bogue, who was attending what proved to be his final dinner and who died on 5 December 1870, bet Mr George Paulin that there would not be a salmon of 40 lb weight brought into the Fish House during season 1869. He lost the wager: one of 48 lb and another of 58 lb were brought in.

Messrs Bowhill and Sanderson exchanged three wagers after dinner in 1869. One of these was that the price of wheat would be higher in 1870 than 1869. The wager was lost by Mr Bowhill because the price was lower by ten shillings per boll. For those of us who know nothing about weights and measures now, let alone in 1869, a boll equalled six English bushels, or 24 pecks, or 48 gallons.

1869 saw the introduction of a new sporting wager. Mr William Miller, who attended dinners for only three years between 1868 and 1870, bet Mr Robert Weddell, who was attending the first of his forty dinners, that Scotland would carry off the Elcho Challenge Shield in 1869 against England and Ireland. The wager was lost by Mr Weddell.

The Elcho is the oldest and most prestigious long-range rifle contest in the world, but its origins and those of the shield are less well known. It derived from the Volunteer Force, which was formed in 1859 in response to the fear of a French invasion. This started in a small way with informal groups and rifle clubs, but such was the enthusiasm that the government authorised the lords lieutenant of each county to organise local corps. Thousands flocked to join because people were keen to participate in the new sport of rifle shooting. There were virtually no rules about danger areas, and it was easy to find suitable sites for target practice.

The Elcho shield

In the late summer of 1859, leaders of the Volunteer movement resolved to further its aims and promote rifle shooting by forming a national association. This would be for 'the encouragement of Volunteer Rifle Corps and the promotion of rifle shooting throughout Great Britain'. In November 1859 a meeting was held with the London Rifle Brigade with the object of forming a National Rifle Association. Lord Elcho, who was a keen Volunteer and supporter of the scheme, wrote to *The Times* on 9 December, setting out the aims of the new association and the plans to hold a great annual national meeting for rifle shooting. The first of these would be in July 1860.

In 1861 Scotland challenged England to a contest. The terms of the challenge pleased Lord Elcho, who had determined to give a prize to the National Rifle Association's annual meeting at Wimbledon. He wished it to be a prize 'for annual competition as an encouragement to International small-bore shooting, and also that my name might be perpetuated in connection with the Association and the volunteers'. He asked his friend George Frederick Watts to design a suitable trophy, and the resulting iron shield (measuring 6 ft x 3 ft) is a triumph of mid-Victorian art. Watts was a well-known and popular artist who had painted many fine portraits, but was perhaps better known for his allegorical and historical scenes.

The first match was contested on 9 July 1862. England won comfortably for the first two years. By 1864, the match was considered as important as the Boat Race, or the Eton versus Harrow match at Lords, and Scotland were the delighted victors by twenty-five points. Though the shield was still a plaster model it was substantial enough for the Scots to carry off in triumph.

On Wednesday 15 February 1871, thirteen members met at the Kings Arms Hotel, with Mr George Paulin in the chair, and Mr Robert Weddell serving as vice chairman. Attending for the first time was Mr Thomas Allan, who was a founder member of the Tweed Salmon Club from 1854 to 1868, and a timber and slate merchant (trading as Allan Brothers). He served as mayor of Berwick in 1861 and was sheriff in 1859 and 1869. Born in 1825, he attended the dinner annually until 1884 when he resigned. He died in 1892. During the evening there were several wagers of interest.

Mr Andrew Thompson bet Dr Henry Richardson a bottle of wine that the supply of water from Tweedmouth Foundry would be in operation by 1 August 1871. The wager was lost by Mr Thompson, since the works were not in operation until 13 October 1871.

Mr Allan, laying his first wager, bet Dr Richardson that the Marchioness of Lorne would give birth to a child by 5 February 1872. He lost this wager.

The marchioness was Princess Louise, who had married Lord Lorne on 21 March 1871. This was the first time a British princess had married a commoner since 1515. Despite opposition particularly from the prince of Wales, Queen Victoria realised that times were changing, and was convinced that marriage outside the traditional royal houses would strengthen the throne both morally and physically.

At age 33, Lord Lorne was Canada's youngest governor-general, but he was not too young to handle the demands of his post. Intensely interested in Canada and Canadians, he travelled throughout the country, encouraging the establishment of numerous institutions. He and Princess Louise made many lasting contributions to Canadian society, especially in the arts and sciences. They encouraged the establishment of the Royal Society of Canada, the Royal Canadian Academy of Arts and the National Gallery of Canada, even selecting some of its first paintings. In addition to acting as a patron of arts and letters in Canada, Lorne was the author of many books of prose and poetry. His writings show a deep appreciation of Canada's physical beauty.

Princess Louise herself was an accomplished writer, sculptor and artist – she painted well in both oils and water colours. A door she painted with sprigs of apple blossoms can still be seen in the Monck wing corridor at Rideau Hall. She gave the name Regina to the capital of Saskatchewan, and both the district of Alberta in the Northwest Territories (later the province of Alberta) and Lake Louise in that district were named after her (Alberta, after her father Prince Albert, was one of her Christian names). Although she was often unwell following a sleigh accident in Ottawa in 1880, she was a compassionate woman and personally nursed the sick during an epidemic of scarlet fever.

Wagers were laid annually between 1869 and 1874 about the fate of David Livingstone. Evidence of the difficulties with communications can be seen in the wager laid by Dr William Jamieson with Mr Thomas Allan that in the course of this year 1874 there would be authentic news that Dr Livingstone was alive. Interestingly, it was lost by Mr Allan because news was received that Dr Livingstone had been alive on 15 February 1874, but died in the month of May 1874. How cruel. Mr Allan should actually have been credited with a win, because later reports showed that in fact Livingstone had died on 1 May 1873.

Livingstone was a Scottish Congregationalist pioneer medical missionary with the London Missionary Society. He became one of the most popular heroes of the late nineteenth century because of his activity as an explorer in Africa. Livingstone completely lost contact with the outside world for six years and was ill for most of the last four years of his life. His meeting with H. M. Stanley in October 1871 gave rise to the popular quotation, 'Dr. Livingstone, I presume?'

After dinner on Thursday 15 February 1872, Dr William Jamieson bet Mr George Paulin that they would have heard that Sir Samuel Baker would have sailed to join the Nianza Expedition. Dr Jamieson lost the wager, largely because of slow communications.

Sir Samuel White Baker, KCB, FRS, FRGS (8 June 1821–30 December 1893) was a British officer who also held the titles of pasha and major-general in the Ottoman Empire and Egypt. He served as the governor-general of the Equatorial Nile (now in southern Sudan and northern Uganda), which he established as the province of Equatoria, between April 1869 and August 1873. He is mostly remembered as the discoverer of Lake Albert (which was known as Albert Nyanza), as an explorer of the Nile and the interior of central Africa, and for his exploits as a big game hunter in Asia, Africa, Europe and North America. Also notable as a naturalist, engineer, writer and abolitionist, Baker wrote a considerable number of books and published articles. He was a friend of King Edward, who as prince of Wales with Princess (later Queen) Alexandra, visited him in Egypt.

One of the most interesting series of wagers in the history of the club was first raised at the 1872 dinner, then reinforced at the 1874 dinner. In 1872 Dr Richardson bet Dr Brown that the claimant in the celebrated Titchborne case would not only fail in establishing his claim to the baronetcy, but that proceedings would be taken against him as an imposter by 5 February 1873. This was lost by Dr Brown because the case went to trial. Then at the 1874 dinner, Mr Stephen Sanderson bet Mr Robert Weddell that the claimant, Arthur Orton (1834–1898), would not be convicted. The wager was lost by Mr Sanderson, since Orton was found guilty on Saturday 28 February 1874. Mr Robert Thompson, attending his second dinner, bet Dr Richardson that the claimant would be sentenced to not less than five years penal servitude, and as we shall see, won his wager.

Sir Roger Charles Doughty Titchborne was born on 5 January 1829 in Paris, the eldest son and heir of a Roman Catholic family from Hampshire. King James I of England had made his ancestor Sir Benjamin Titchborne, sheriff of Southampton, a baronet in 1621. His father was James Francis Doughty-Titchborne, and his mother the French-born Henriette Felicite.

Through the influence of his mother, who did not appreciate England greatly, the boy mainly spoke French. He lived with his mother in France until the age of 16. His father had to claim that he needed to attend a funeral in England before his mother would let him leave France. In 1849 he went to Stonyhurst College, and later that year he joined the 6th Dragoon Guards in Dublin. Apparently his French accent caused ridicule, and he sold his commission in 1852. Next year he left for South America. From Valparaíso he crossed the Andes and arrived in Rio de Janeiro in 1854. In April, on his way back home, his ship was lost at sea with all hands, and he was pronounced dead the next year. The title and the estates passed to his younger brother, Sir Alfred Joseph Doughty-Titchborne (who died in 1866).

Sir Roger's mother refused to accept that he was dead. She sent inquiries all over the world, and in November 1865 she received a letter from a Sydney lawyer who claimed that a man supposedly fitting the description of her son was living as a butcher in Wagga Wagga, Australia.

The supposed Sir Roger was actually Arthur Orton, who at the time used the name Tom Castro. Instead of sharp features and black hair, he had round features and light brown hair. He was also overweight and did not speak a word of French. His first letter referred to facts Lady Titchborne did not recognise. However, Lady Titchborne was desperate enough to accept him as her son, and sent him money to come to her.

Orton was reluctant to go at first, presumably because he feared exposure, but his associates – one of whom was an old friend of Sir Roger's father – changed his mind. Sir Roger's former servant Andrew Bogle accompanied him on his trip to Britain. He arrived in London on Christmas Day 1866, and visited the Titchborne estates. There he met the Titchborne family solicitor Edward Hopkins and Francis J. Baigent, who became his supporters. When in January he travelled to the Paris hotel where Lady Titchborne was living, the desperate lady 'recognised' him instantly as her son. She even handed him Sir Roger's letters from South America. The fact that Orton did not understand a word of French did not bother her, and she gave him an allowance of £1,000 a year. Orton researched Sir Roger's life to reinforce his imposture.

After Lady Titchborne's acceptance, various other acquaintances of Sir Roger accepted him as well. They included other officers of the 6th Dragoons, several county families and Hampshire villagers. He even hired a group of manservants who had served in the 6th Dragoon Guards.

Other members of the Titchborne family were not so gullible. Their investigators found out that Orton was a butcher's son from Wapping. He had jumped ship in Valparaíso, Chile, where he had taken the name Castro from a friendly family. Orton had even inquired about his family members in Wapping when he came back from Australia. They also found many other discrepancies when Orton tried to fit his own South American experiences to those of Sir Roger.

When Lady Titchborne died in March 1868, Orton lost his most prominent supporter. He might well have stopped the charade had he not owed a significant amount of money to his creditors. (He sold 'Titchborne Bonds' to pay the legal costs when he tried to claim his inheritance from the Titchborne family.) The rightful heir at the time, Sir Henry Alfred Joseph Doughty-Titchborne, was only two years old.

Orton's criminal trial began in 1873 and lasted 188 days, with the judge, Sir Alexander Cockburn, taking 18 days to sum up. His defence was led by Edward Kenealy, who would later be disbarred for his aggressive behaviour during the case. Testimony by Orton's former girlfriend, among others, convinced the jury that he was not Sir Roger. Orton was convicted on two counts of perjury, and was sentenced to fourteen years' hard labour. The legal costs amounted to £200,000 (at least £10 million in modern terms).

Many people who had supported the claimant's efforts refused to accept the verdict, and claimed that Orton had been unjustly persecuted.

The rumours included conspiracy theories involving Jesuits. Kenealy was elected to Parliament, but failed to convince other members to take the Titchborne case to a Royal Commission in April 1875. As a result, Orton's supporters started a small-scale riot in London. Several thousand people marched in Hyde Park in support of Orton on 29 March 1875.

Orton served ten years in prison and was released in 1884, by which time the public had forgotten him. He died in poverty on 2 April 1898. His coffin still carries the name Sir Roger Charles Doughty Titchborne.

There is a really interesting postscript, for this case was the inspiration for Anthony Trollope's novel *Is He Popinjoy?* Trollope wrote it between 12 October 1874 and 3 May 1875, making his protagonist the claimant to the title Lord Popinjoy. He was certain that Orton was an imposter, but he left England by boat on 1 March 1875 bound for Australia, and was effectively incommunicado when the verdict was announced. In consequence, unusually for Trollope, he gave an ambiguous ending to his account.

Wagers laid after dinner in 1875 and 1876 focused almost exclusively on fishing, sport and politics, all reported in a different form later in this book. On the twenty-fifth anniversary of the first dinner, only two of the original members were present: Mr Alexander Lowrey and Mr James Weddell, whose son Robert became a member in 1869. That evening a rare weather wager was made by Dr Colville Brown, who was a member from 1869 to 1881. He bet Dr William Jamieson that there would be snow in Berwick on Christmas Day 1876. Dr Jamieson lost because it snowed that morning.

The social whirl of Berwick was the subject of a wager laid after dinner in 1877. Mr Thomas Allan bet Mr Andrew Thompson that the Bachelors' Ball would take place in April next and that not less than 200 would attend it. Mr Allan lost: the bachelors of Berwick and neighbourhood did host an excellent ball on 6 April 1877, though only about 150 attended. Nevertheless, it seems the ball must have prospered because it was the subject of another wager in 1882 when Mr Blake Weatherhead bet Mr James Nicholson that the cost of the Bachelors' Ball at Belford on 17th inst. would not be under £5 per subscribing bachelor. The wager was lost by Mr Weatherhead, since the price was between £4 and £5.

The theme continued. Mr Allan bet Mr John Logan that five of the guarantors of the last Berwick Bachelors' Ball would be married by 1 February 1883. Mr Allan lost because only four of them married. Arguably the ball was achieving its objective. Further wagers about the ticket price were repeated in 1883 and 1887, when Mr Edward Willoby Junior (his father Mr Edward Willoby Senior had been a member from

1850 to 1882) bet Mr Logan that the price per head for the Bachelors' Ball for 1887 would be lower than in 1886. Mr Willoby lost because in 1886 the price was £2.14/- and in 1887 £2.17/-. To contemporary eyes, this looks dead cheap, but the purchasing power of one pound sterling in 1890 equated to £57.56 in 2004.

In the early 1880s we have a glimpse of the development of Berwick town and the surrounding area. In 1880 Mr Edward Willoby bet Captain Francis Norman that the sewering of Castle Terrace would not be commenced by 5 February 1881. Mr Willoby lost because it began in November 1880.

The following year Dr Brown lost two wagers on local building projects. First he bet Mr Willoby that the new Norham Water Works would be commenced by 5 February 1882. He then bet Mr Paulin that there would be another dwelling house commenced in Castle Terrace by 5 February 1882. Following Dr Brown's lead, in 1882 Mr Logan bet Mr Willoby that the Norham Water Works would not be begun by 5 February 1883. Mr Willoby lost.

1882 was marked by some new-style wagers. For example, Mr Henry Peters, who attended the dinner for 25 years until he died in May 1907, and was sheriff of Berwick in 1890, bet Mr William Hindmarsh that the Cloture rules would not be passed by the House of Commons in its 1882 session.

The Cloture rules addressed any procedure for limiting or curtailing debate in a legislature, forcing the matter to a vote even when there were members still wanting to speak. One form in the United Kingdom is the 'guillotine' resolution which restricts discussion on the remaining clauses of a government bill. The rule is used to save parliamentary time by preventing filibusters. Mr Peters lost the original wager plus a second one with Mr Hindmarsh, who bet that the rules would be passed by a majority of at least twenty; they were passed by a majority of at least sixty.

Mr Peters was on stronger ground when he bet Mr Robert Weddell that the Government would release Mr Parnell, MP, within three months from the date of the dinner. Weddell lost: he was released on 4 May.

Charles Stewart Parnell (27 June 1846–6 October 1891) was an Irish landowner, nationalist political leader, land reform agitator, and founder and leader of the Irish Parliamentary Party. He was one of the most important figures in nineteenth-century Ireland, and described by prime minister William Gladstone as the most remarkable person he had ever met. Parnell led his party as member of Parliament through the period of

Irish nationalism between 1875 and his death in 1891. The future Liberal prime minister, H. H. Asquith, described him as one of the three or four greatest men of the nineteenth century, while Lord Haldane described him as the strongest man the British House of Commons had seen in 150 years. The Irish Parliamentary Party split during 1890, following revelations of Parnell's private life which impinged on his political career.

Parnell's own newspaper, *United Ireland*, attacked the Second Irish Land Act 1881, and he was arrested on 13 October 1881 together with his party lieutenants, William O'Brien, John Dillon, Michael Davitt and Willie Redmond, who had also conducted a bitter verbal offensive. They were imprisoned under a proclaimed Coercion Act in Kilmainham Gaol for 'sabotaging the Land Act'. His release in May marked a critical turning point in the development of Parnell's leadership, and he subsequently returned to the parameters of parliamentary and constitutional politics.

Men had spent many years trying to perfect flight by hot air balloon, but 1882 saw the first wager on the subject when Mr James Nicholson, who only attended four dinners and who died in 1887, bet Dr Henry Richardson that 'the Aeronauts' would safely cross the English Channel on their first trial after the dinner. Mr Nicholson lost.

In March 1882 Joseph Simmons and Colonel Brine attempted to cross the English Channel from Canterbury to France. The take-off was watched by several thousand people. They flew successfully across Dover, but when they were eight miles off Calais the wind veered. They realised they were liable to drift over the North Sea, so Simmons decided to ditch in the Channel, where fortunately they were picked up by a fishing vessel.

Undaunted, in June 1882 Simmons planned to fly by balloon to France with Sir Claude Champion de Crespigny. The launch from Maldon was clumsily executed, with the assistants holding on to one side of the basket for too long. The basket was flung against a wall and one spectator was crushed, sustaining broken ribs. Sir Claude was thrown from the basket and suffered a broken leg, cracked ribs and concussion. Simmons was struck on the head but managed to remain in the basket. He bravely decided to continue the flight, and achieved his goal by landing in a field near Arras.

In August 1888, Simmons with two companions, Horace Field, a photographer from Brighton, and Henry Alexander Miers, an assistant at the Natural History Museum, took off from the Olympia exhibition in London. They intended to cross the English Channel and ultimately aimed to reach Vienna. The winds turned unfavourable and they followed the Great Eastern Railway line as far as Witham. Simmons then decided to abandon the attempt and land.

At first there were too many houses in the area to land, but he identified a barley field in Ulting near to Turner's beer house which seemed to be suitable as a landing spot. A newspaper later disparagingly described it as 'bleak spot'. As they tried to land, a grappling iron was thrown out but failed to connect with the ground and became entangled in a tree. The balloon hit the ground, bounced two or three times and then burst, so the basket plunged to the ground.

Two witnesses, Frederick Cramner, a labourer from nearby Hatfield Peverel, and William Baker, a blacksmith, ran to assist the efforts to control the balloon, but their attempts were in vain. PC Claxton from nearby Woodham Water also saw the balloon come down, and went to the scene. Simmons died on site. Field and Miers were both badly injured and taken to a nearby house, from where they later gave evidence to the coroner and a jury.

The murder in Phoenix Park, Dublin, on 6 May 1882 of Lord Frederick Cavendish, the newly appointed chief secretary for Ireland, and Thomas Henry Burke, the permanent under secretary, the most senior Irish civil servant, produced two wagers on 15 February 1883. Cavendish, who had worked as Gladstone's private secretary and was married to his niece, had arrived in Ireland on the very day that he was murdered. Superintendent John Mallon, a Catholic who came from Armagh, led the investigation and had a pretty shrewd idea of who was involved. A large number of former Fenian activists were arrested, and the police kept them in prison by claiming they were connected with other crimes. By playing off one suspect against another Mallon got several of them to reveal what they knew.

First Mr Edward Willoby bet Mr Stephen Sanderson that Councillor James Carey of Dublin would be hanged by operation of law before 5 February 1884. Mr Willoby lost because Carey turned Queen's evidence and testified against his co-conspirators. Joe Brady, Michael Fagan, Thomas Caffrey, Dan Curley and Tim Kelly were convicted of the murder and were hanged by William Marwood in Kilmainham Gaol in Dublin between 14 May and 4 June 1883. Others were sentenced to serve long prison terms.

Although his evidence saved him from hanging, Carey's life was in danger from supporters of the men he had sent to the gallows. He, his wife and family were secretly put on board the *Kinfauns Castle*, bound for the Cape of Good Hope. They sailed on 6 July under the name of Power. On board the same ship was one Patrick O'Donnell, a bricklayer, who became friendly with Carey. After stopping off in Cape Town, he was informed by chance who his new friend really was. O'Donnell chose to continue his journey with Carey, on board the *Melrose* which was bound from Cape Town to Natal. When the vessel was 12 miles off Cape Vaccas, on 29 July 1883, O'Donnell shot Carey dead. He was brought to England, tried and found guilty of murder, and executed at Newgate on 17 December.

In the second wager, Mr Thomas Allan bet Mr Robert Bolam that seven or more persons would be hanged for the murder of Lord Cavendish and Mr Bourke. Allan lost because only five were hanged.

The last unusual wager of 1883 was between Captain Francis Norman and Mr Robert Bolam, that the Deceased Wife's Sister's Bill would not have passed the House of Lords by 5 February 1884.

The Deceased Wife's Sister's Marriage Act was actually not passed until 1907 after some 50 years of vigorous public debate into the moral and legal challenges of marrying the surviving sister of one's late wife, so Mr Bolam lost. Although the Act removed the prohibition, it allowed individual clergy to refuse to conduct marriages which would previously have been prohibited. It did exactly what it said and no more, and it was not until 1921 that the Deceased Brother's Widow's Marriage Act 1921 was passed. The Marriage (Prohibited Degrees) Relationship Act 1931 extended the operation of the 1907 Act to allow the marriages of nieces and nephews by marriage as well.

The meeting of the club on 15 February 1884 started on a sombre note:

> On the motion of Dr Richardson, seconded by the Chairman, it was unanimously agreed to record in the Minutes the great loss which the Club had suffered by the death of the late Mr James Weddell, and the deep sympathy which the members feel for his family in the bereavement they have sustained; also the high esteem which the Club entertained of the kindly general manner in which Mr Weddell discharged during a period of upwards of 40 years his duties as Honorary Secretary, and the zeal and urbanity he invariably displayed while holding that office. It was also resolved to forward an extract of this Minute to Mr Robert Weddell.

Poor Mr Robert Weddell may not have been as excited by the news that the members then unanimously elected him as the new honorary secretary.

Aside from the traditional wagers that evening, there was one scandal for members to trade with each other. Mr John Weatherhead bet Mr Thomas Allan that the Fortescue and Garmoyle case would never come to trial. At the same time, Mr Robert Thompson bet Mr Alexander Lowrey that the damages in the trial would not exceed £10,000. Mr Weatherhead lost the first bet and Mr Lowrey the second.

Miss Fortescue, a well-educated young lady, had turned to the stage after the failure of her father's business. During 1882 she met and became increasingly involved with Lord Garmoyle, the son of Earl Cairns, who eventually proposed to her with his family's cautious consent. They did express reservations about her profession, but everyone agreed that she was 'a highly modest and high-minded English gentlewoman'. But without warning, on 21 January 1884 Garmoyle wrote to his fiancée to break off the engagement. In a move designed to uphold her reputation, Miss Fortescue decided she had to take the matter to court. Breach of an agreement to marry was actionable in those days, and there was no contest from the defendant, who willingly accepted that he had broken his contract and offered to pay compensation of £10,000. (£10,000 in 1884 was roughly equal in purchasing power to £500,000 in 2010.)

On Monday 16 February 1885 fifty-two wagers were laid by the fifteen members who attended the dinner. The sheriff of Berwick, Captain Norman, bet Mr John Weatherhead, his under-sheriff, that the recorder would receive a pair of white gloves at the next year's Quarter Sessions. This referred to an interesting and very ancient tradition. When judges made a circuit of ancient English towns to hold assizes, any town which had no criminals to be tried celebrated the 'maiden assize' by presenting the judges with white gloves. One theory is that judges were not allowed to wear gloves on the bench, so to give a judge a pair of gloves symbolised that he need not take his seat. In 1634 a highwayman called Cavell was acquitted of his crime and wrote a dedication 'to all the impartial judges of His Majesties Bench, my Lord Chiefe Justice and his other three honourable Assistants, those pardoned men, who taste their Princes loves (as married to new life) do give you gloves'. The wearing of white gloves has always been symbolic of having clean hands, and plays a large part in Masonic tradition. The wager was lost by Captain Norman because the court had one criminal case and two rating appeals.

Mr David Herriot, attending his first dinner, bet Mr James Nicholson who, by chance was attending his last dinner, that Lord Durham would not succeed in obtaining a divorce.

Lord Durham, who had sown plenty of wild oats in his youth, had been exhorted by his family to settle down. In 1882 he briefly courted, then swiftly married Miss Ethel Milner, who was the sister of the Hon. Mrs Gerard, a well-known society beauty. Within days – if not hours – the noble lord was questioning his own actions because his bride proved to be exceptionally shy and almost mute. He claimed that she was an imbecile, while others said she was insane. Lord Durham sued for divorce on the grounds that Lady Durham must have been insane before they married. He claimed that he had never seen his fiancée alone, so the whole affair was based upon a lie. Very worthy witnesses appeared for both sides in the case, with the Archbishop of York saying that he had met Miss Milner before her marriage, and that she was perfectly able to converse one to one but was more reserved in company. The petition was dismissed because the judge ruled that there was no way to measure her madness, and in any event, it was not a sufficient reason to break a sacred matrimonial tie. So Mr Herriot won his bet.

Sticking with the work of the courts, Dr Thomas Fraser bet Mr John Weatherhead that James Gilbert Cunningham would not be convicted for any of the offences with which he was charged in connection with causing an explosion at the Tower of London in January 1885. Cunningham was tried at the Central Criminal Court on 18 May 1885. He was found guilty and sentenced to penal servitude for life, so Dr Fraser lost. *Lloyds Weekly News* published an image of the defendant, which was taken from the first photograph ever supplied to the press by the Metropolitan Police. Half-tone reproduction of photographs was not possible at the time, so Alfred Bryan made a sketch of it.

On puckish form, Mr Henry Peters bet Mr James Nicholson that he would not find a word to rhyme with Timbuctoo (which Mr Peters had not heard before) by 5 February 1886. Mr Nicholson lost. Fair revenge perhaps, because it was he who in 1883 had bet Dr Henry Richardson that he would not be able to find a word in the English language (proper names excepted) to rhyme with 'orange'. Dr Richardson lost that bet, which must have been read out by the chairman, Richard Landale, one hundred years later on the night of 15 February 1983 at the Turret House Hotel. Mr Michael Lyndon Skeggs promptly made the same bet with Mr David Hotham, who also lost.

Today the press pays almost no attention to divorce cases, but in the late nineteenth century the public still enjoyed a mildly malicious thrill on learning of the marriage difficulties of the nobility and other public figures. The diners on 15 February 1886 were exercised by the political and married career of Sir Charles Dilke, Bt.

Dilke became Liberal member of Parliament for Chelsea in 1868. He was parliamentary under-secretary of state for foreign affairs from 1880 to 1882 during Gladstone's second government, and was admitted to the Privy Council in 1882. In December 1882 he entered the cabinet as president of the Local Government Board, serving until 1885. A leading and determined radical within the Liberal Party, he negotiated the passage of the Third Reform Act, which the Conservatives allowed through the House of Lords in return for a redistribution of seats which was favourable to themselves. (The granting of the vote to agricultural labourers threatened Conservative dominance of rural seats, but in return many double-member seats were abolished and the seats redistributed to suburbia, where Conservative support was growing.) He also supported laws giving the municipal franchise to women, legalising labour unions, improving working conditions and limiting working hours, as well as being one of the earliest campaigners for universal schooling.

Dilke started an affair with Ellen Eustace Smith, the mother of his brother's new bride, May. The relationship continued after his own marriage in 1884. In July 1885 he was accused of seducing Virginia, the younger daughter of Thomas and Ellen Eustace Smith, in the first year of her marriage to Donald Crawford MP. This was supposed to have occurred in 1882 when Virginia was nineteen, and she claimed that the affair had continued on an irregular basis for the next two and a half years. Crawford sued for divorce, and the case was heard on 12 February 1886 before the Hon. Mr Justice Butt in the Probate, Divorce and Admiralty Division. Virginia Crawford was not in court and the sole evidence was her husband's account of her confession. There were also some accounts by servants, which were both circumstantial and insubstantial.

Dilke, aware of his vulnerability over his affair with Virginia's mother, refused to give evidence, largely on the advice of his confidante Joseph Chamberlain. Butt found – paradoxically – that Virginia had been guilty of adultery with Dilke, but that there was no admissible evidence that Dilke had been guilty of adultery with Virginia. Concluding that 'I cannot see any case whatsoever against Sir Charles Dilke', he dismissed Dilke from the suit with costs, and pronounced a decree nisi dissolving the Crawfords' marriage.

This paradoxical finding left doubts hanging over Dilke's respectability, and investigative journalist William Thomas Stead launched a public campaign against him. Two months later, in April, Dilke sought to reopen the case and clear his name by making the Queen's proctor a party to the case and opposing the decree absolute. Unfortunately, Dilke and his legal team badly miscalculated. They had planned to subject Virginia to a searching cross-examination, but since Dilke had been dismissed from the case he had no locus standi and was unable to call her as a witness. As a consequence it was Dilke himself who was subjected to severe scrutiny in the witness box by Henry Matthews. Matthews' attack was devastating, and Dilke proved an unconvincing witness. His habit of cutting pieces out of his diary with scissors was held up to particular ridicule, as it created the impression that he had cut out evidence of potentially embarrassing appointments. The jury found that Virginia had presented the true version of the facts, and that the decree absolute should be granted.

Dilke was ruined. Other women claimed he had approached them for a liaison. Various lurid rumours circulated about his love-life, including that he had invited a maidservant to join himself and his lover in bed, and that he had introduced one or more women to 'every kind of French vice'. For a time it seemed that he would be tried for perjury, although this did not happen. The accusations had a devastating effect on his political career, leading eventually to the loss of his parliamentary seat in the 1886 UK general election. Matthews, on the other hand, gained public acclaim, winning the seat of Birmingham East as a Conservative at the same election. Queen Victoria, who approved of his performance in the trial, demanded that he be included in Lord Salisbury's cabinet, and he was made home secretary.

Dilke spent much of the remainder of his life and much of his fortune trying to exonerate himself, which adds a little weight to the view that Virginia had lied about the identity of her lover. Various men have been implicated over the years, including Archibald Primrose, Fifth Earl of Rosebery, and Chamberlain himself.

Extraordinarily, Dilke later became MP for the Forest of Dean in 1892, serving until his death in 1911. He hoped to be appointed secretary of state for war in the Liberal Government formed in 1905, but this was not to be.

In 1886 Mr John Weatherhead bet Mr Stephen Sanderson that Dilke would not be one of HM ministers on 5 February 1887. Mr Weatherhead won because Dilke was defeated at the General Election of 1886 by Mr Whitmore by 176 votes. At the same time Dr Thomas Fraser bet Mr David Herriot that Dilke would not be an MP on 5 February 1887. Mr Herriot lost. And finally Mr Henry Peters bet Mr Robert Weddell that the Queen's proctor would intervene in the case of *Crawford* v. *Dilke*. Mr Weddell lost because the proctor did intervene.

Dilke's later electoral success was recorded in a wager between Mr Peters and Captain Francis Norman on the night of 15 February 1892, that he would become a member of the British House of Commons on 5 February 1893. Captain Norman lost because Dilke was duly elected.

Local interests were recorded by Mr Evan Sanderson, who bet Mr Robert Weddell that by 5 February 1887 the new railway from Alnwick to Cornhill would be opened for general traffic. Mr Sanderson lost. A similar bet was laid in 1887, when Mr William Hindmarsh bet Mr Edward Willoby Senior that the new Alnwick & Cornhill Railway would not be open for general traffic by 1 August 1887. Mr Willoby lost, because the railway opened for general traffic on 5 September 1887

Dr Thomas Fraser bet Mr Edward Willoby Junior, who was attending his first dinner in 1886 and who would remain a member for thirty-five years, that during the next winter there would be no curling at the local curling pond before 15 December. Dr Fraser lost because there was curling on 2 December 1886.

Dr Thomas Fraser bet Mr David Herriot that the Industrial Exhibition to be opened in Edinburgh would not pay its expenses. Dr Fraser lost because the exhibition made a healthy profit.

This was one of a series of exhibitions, set up under the presidency of the then prince of Wales, and managed by Sir Cunliffe Owen, which had commenced at South Kensington in 1883. The first was devoted to a display of the various industries connected with fishing; the second, in 1884, to objects connected with hygiene; the third, in 1885, to inventions; and the fourth, in 1886, to the British colonies and India. These exhibitions attracted a large number of visitors and realised a substantial profit. They might have been continued indefinitely if it had not been that the buildings in which they were held became very dilapidated, and the ground covered by them was required for other purposes.

The Crystal Palace held a successful International Exhibition in 1884, and there was an Italian Exhibition at Turin, and a Forestry Exhibition at Edinburgh, during the same year. A World's Industrial Fair was held at New Orleans in 1884–1885, and there were universal Exhibitions at Montenegro and Antwerp in 1885, at Edinburgh in 1886, Liverpool, Adelaide, Newcastle and Manchester in 1887, and at Glasgow, Barcelona and Brussels in 1888. Melbourne held an International Exhibition in 1888– 1889 to celebrate the Centenary of Australia.

The records show that it was on the night of 15 February 1887 that Captain Francis Norman proposed that in addition to the usual Loyal Toast, and the health of the new members (if any), 'Success to the salmon fishings in the Tweed' should be added to the list and become the vice-chairman's toast. The motion was carried, and this toast, although somewhat modified over time, remains the vice-chairman's toast today.

Captain Francis Norman, member 1882–1910

4
1890–1914

The club records are sadly incomplete because somewhere along the line at least one minute book was mislaid. This means that we have no hard evidence of what went on between 1894 and 1903 – a real loss, since this covered the end of the Victorian era and the Boer War. There are no documents for the period 1915–1919 because the club did not meet then, or between 1940 and 1945. A photo album commissioned at the business meeting in 1891 disappeared in the 1970s and was presumed lost for good. Happily it was produced by the King's Own Scottish Borders Museum on 30 November 2011 during a day of research by the author into the biographies of members who had served in the regiment. It seems that when Lt Col Philip Harrison died, it was among his possessions and was quietly filed in the regimental archives.

We can deduce that the following people were elected to the club between 1894 and 1903, because the minutes for 1904 show them attending, but without any commentary on recent election:

> Lt Col Francis Douglas Blake, who resigned in 1905, received a baronetcy in 1907, served as the MP for Berwick and as vice lord lieutenant of the county 1920 1931
> Mr William Bolam
> Captain John Evelyn Carr
> Mr Adam Darling
> Mr Frederick Henderson
> Mr Henry Richardson (who is not to be confused with the older Henry Richardson, who was a member from 1865 until he died in October 1885)
> Rev. W. M. Smythe, who is said to have been elected in 1900
> Mr Joseph Tiffen, who is said to have been elected in 1897.

Those who resigned or died during the missing years were:

> Mr Robert Bolam
> Mr George Paulin, who attended his first dinner in 1862. Over his recorded thirty-one years of membership he laid seventy-seven wagers, received sixty-eight and lost seventy-four. Most

of his bets were to do with fishing, politics and the dividend of
local companies.
Mr Evan Sanderson
Mr Blake Weatherhead.

The club met on Saturday 15 February 1890 at the Kings Arms with
Captain Norman in the chair. After receiving the apologies of those not
able to attend, the members unanimously elected Mr George Paulin as
the honorary treasurer in place of the late Mr Alexander Lowrey. They
elected Mr James Mein as a new member to fill Mr Lowrey's place, but
they also decided that Sir William Crossman should no longer be considered a member of the club, having failed to attend the last two annual
meetings.

Mr Stephen Sanderson, the new senior member of the club (having
joined in 1857), most feelingly alluded to the loss which the club had
sustained through the death of Mr Lowrey, till then the senior member,
and the extreme sorrow felt by the members at the death of such an old
and esteemed friend. The toast of 'his memory' was drunk in solemn
silence. It was agreed that the chairman should write to Mrs Lowrey and
convey to her the kindly sympathy which the members of the club felt
with her at the loss which all had sustained. Mr Lowrey had been one
of the original members of the club and had acted as honorary treasurer
since 1846.

Only forty wagers were laid that night, and they were very much along
traditional lines. They covered sport (twelve), politics (five), farming
(three), fishing (seven), business (two) and a small range of miscellaneous
bets on issues of local and national interest.

It would be easy to miss the single mention of an unusual tradition. Dr
Charles Fraser bet Mr George Bolam that either the mayor or sheriff of
the borough would be entitled to apply to the town council for a 'silver
cradle' during the ensuing twelve months.

The custom of presenting a miniature silver cradle to a local politician
when his wife gave birth to a child while her husband was in office was
quite widespread for some time in New Zealand, Canada, the USA and
Britain. The earliest known New Zealand-made cradle of this type was
crafted in 1868 in the Dunedin workshop of John Hislop for presentation
to the mayoress of Alexandra. Dr Fraser lost the bet.

There was a particularly interesting wager between Dr Thomas Fraser
and Mr Blake Weatherhead that the census return of the population for
the borough of Berwick upon Tweed in 1891 would be less than 1881. Dr
Fraser won. In 1881 the population was 13,998, and in 1891, 13,347.

There is much more to this than meets the eye. In 1296 King Edward I, infuriated by Berwick espousing allegiance to Scotland, ransacked the town over the course of three days, killing more than 8,000 people in the process. This represented half the population of the town, which never recovered. At the time, it was one of the premier trading ports in England, enjoying prosperous business with Holland. Indeed, a large number of Flemish traders were killed during the slaughter. The 2001 census showed that the population of the town was 11,665, although the borough as a whole boasted 25,949, so the decline which started with such ferocity more than 700 years ago continues apace.

Dr Fraser bet Mr Evan Sanderson that Sir William Gordon-Cumming would obtain a verdict in the forthcoming baccarat case. Dr Fraser lost.

This was a famous case. In September 1890, Gordon-Cumming was invited, along with the prince of Wales, to a house party at Tranby Croft in Yorkshire. There he was accused of cheating at baccarat and compelled to sign a confession and an undertaking never to play cards again. Rumours of the incident circulated and he found himself shunned by smart society. In an attempt to restore his honour, he sued some of those present at Tranby Croft for defamation, calling Prince Edward as a witness. Gordon-Cumming lost and Prince Edward's wrath ensured his total social ostracism.

An important wager about the civic affairs of the town and borough was recorded by Mr Henry Peters. He bet Mr Sanderson that there would be at least twenty-seven subscribers to the proposed sheriff's chain. The wager was lost by Mr Sanderson because there were thirty-four subscribers.

Another important landmark in the history of the Berwick Salmon Club was proposed that night. It was agreed on the motion of Dr Fraser, seconded by Captain Francis Norman, that an album should be obtained for the purpose of recording photographs of past and present members of the club. The honorary treasurer and the honorary secretary were to form a subcommittee for the purpose of carrying out this task. It was also agreed after some little discussion that any member desirous of having a duplicate of such album might procure the same at his own cost. This is the album that disappeared for many years then was rediscovered, and the images it contains now form part of this history.

Fourteen members attended dinner in the Kings Arms Hotel on the night of 15 February 1892. Captain Norman, Mr Mein and Mr Hindmarsh wrote to apologise, which Mr George Bolam, who was also absent, failed to do. Mr Hindmarsh had not attended a dinner since 1887, having moved from the area, and his letter of apology included his formal resignation.

Mr James Richardson Black was welcomed to his first dinner, but he was to prove an ephemeral member because he resigned after attending his second dinner in 1893.

Mr Henry Peters bet Mr Stephen Sanderson that with subscriptions and the result of the bazaar for the Spittal Improvement Fund, the committee would take gross the sum of £2,000. The wager was lost by Mr Peters, since the gross sum taken was £1,807.3.11 (the equivalent of £103,000 in 2009).

A couple of wagers concerned the Osborne, or pearl, case, which was reported in English-speaking newspapers around the world. Indeed, this report is based upon articles in the *Ashburton Guardian* of Auckland, New Zealand and the *Brisbane Courier*.

In February 1891, Miss Ethel Elliott was residing with her sister and brother-in-law at the Boltons in South Kensington. On a visit to see a distant cousin, one Mrs Hargreave, in Torquay she was shown some valuable diamonds and pearls, which were concealed in Mrs Hargreaves' bedroom. Miss Elliott left Torquay to return to London on 18 February, and the following day a young woman of 'ladylike' appearance sold some pearls to a goldsmith and jeweller, Spink, in Gracechurch Street. She gave an address and said that her name was Price. Spink sought to confirm her identity by searching a London directory. They found that someone of a different name lived at the given address, but they accepted her explanation that she was only staying there briefly because she lived in Bradford.

The woman received a crossed cheque for £550, which she then tried to cash at a bank. The bank refused to accept it, so she returned to Spink on 23 February to ask for an open cheque, which the firm duly gave her. By this time, Mrs Hargreave had discovered that her pearls had been stolen, and informed the police, who traced the pearls to Spink. Major and Mrs Hargreave promptly set about suing Spink for the return of the pearls. The police secured a photograph of Miss Elliott, whom Spink identified as the person who had sold the pearls to them.

Meanwhile, Miss Elliott had married a Captain Osborne of the Carabiniers, and in an attempt to stave off the loss of her reputation, she decided somewhat foolishly to sue the Hargreave family for slander. The case went to the High Court, and in the course of the hearing, it became clear that Miss Elliott/Mrs Osborne had indeed sold the pearls. Sir Charles Russell, who was acting for her, threw up the case after discussion with Captain Osborne. She beat a retreat to France, but her husband promptly set off after her and brought her back to England to face the music.

A charge was laid against her of acting under false pretences, but curiously this was dropped because the prosecution offered no evidence. A charge of perjury was however pursued. Mr Sanderson bet Mr John Weatherhead that Mrs Osborne would not get less than eighteen months of penal servitude, and lost the wager. That same evening Dr Collier bet Mr Edward Willoby that Mrs Osborne would not get more than six months, and he too lost. In fact Mrs Osborne was sentenced to nine months imprisonment for perjury. We do not know what became of the Osborne marriage.

We are fortunate to have been kept abreast of technological developments in Berwick, thanks to Mr George Paulin who bet Mr Robert Weddell that electric light would have been introduced into the town of Berwick by a merchant by 15 February 1893. Mr Weddell lost: Murphy's Galloping Horses were enabled for electric light.

On the national stage, Captain Francis Norman bet Dr Thomas Fraser that income tax would be reduced by a penny in the pound in the next budget. Captain Norman, who seems to have been a sporting character who took his consistent losses with good grace, lost again. Tax remained at sixpence in the pound, where it had been since 1888.

A year later, Dr Thomas Fraser bet Mr Edward Willoby that before 5 February 1894 no further lots on the Castle Hills building sites (being developed by Askews) would have been sold. Mr Willoby lost.

Sporting interests were recorded when Mr Mein bet Captain Norman that if Charlie Mitchell and James J. Corbett came together in a pugilistic encounter, Corbett would win. If there was no fight, both would pay. Pretty much as usual, Captain Norman lost.

The contestants fought at Jacksonville on 25 January 1894, and Corbett knocked out Mitchell in three rounds. This was a coup for Corbett, who had faced sustained criticism from the press over his desire to seek title fights only once a year. On 23 January 1893, the *New York Times* wrote a full article about Corbett, who justified his desired schedule of contests on the basis that John L. Sullivan, who had been champion for twelve years, had only ever fought four men. He boldly stated that his preference was to take on Mitchell, who had never been defeated, but if Mitchell would not meet him, he would take on Peter Jackson 'or any man in the world, barring no colour or nationality'.

Mr Robert Bolam bet Mr David Herriot that the Government would not have issued an order for the evacuation of Uganda by 5 February 1894. Mr Herriot lost, but what was going on?

In 1890 a treaty was signed between Great Britain and Germany giving

Britain rights over Buganda. Although the country was perceived to be friendly, peaceful and beautiful, there was considerable tension between religious groups, and on 25 January 1892 the Battle of Mengo took place between Catholics and Anglicans outside modern-day Kampala. The British East Africa Company's local agent, Frederick Lugard, used the company's influence to help the Anglicans to overcome the Catholics, and in 1893 the Union Jack was finally raised in the capital of the country. Hilariously, British bureaucrats mistakenly dropped the B from Buganda and announced that 'Uganda' was the most recent addition to the British Empire.

We leap forward now to 1904, having lost more than ten years of the club's records. The world was a different place. News travelled faster, ordinary people were beginning to own motor cars, Japan was at war with Russia and Dr Tom Fraser was sufficiently concerned to bet Mr David Herriot that the urinals (or one of them) on the bridge to Tweed-mouth would have been removed by 5 February 1905. Dr Fraser lost. Public lavatories were also the subject of another wager between Mr Henry Richardson Junior, who was attending his final dinner, who bet Mr Joseph Tiffen that the takings at the ladies' lavatory on Bank Hill would exceed £7 during the current financial year. Mr Richardson lost: the takings were £6.12.

At the same time, Captain John Evelyn Carr bet Mr Henry Parker in his absence that the galleries in the parish church would be pulled down by 5 February 1905. The bet was lost by Mr Parker: the galleries were down by 30 January 1905.

Mr Parker failed to attend many dinners. The records show that year after year he wrote to apologise for being absent. Wagers were made in his name, but his first attendance is shown in 1910. He missed dinner in 1911 and his final dinner was in 1912. His resignation was accepted in 1914. This attitude to the affairs of the Club was discussed on 15 February 1906. After much debate, it was agreed that any member who went abroad and who did not attend the annual meeting of the club for two successive years without a cause which was satisfactory to the members should ipso facto cease to be a member.

Mr William Bolam attended his first dinner in 1904 and continued as a member of the club until 1934. He was the author of a new style of wager which allows us for the first time to picture what members looked like. He bet Mr Frederick Henderson that he, Bolam, was at least two inches taller than any other member present. Mr Bolam proved to be 6 ft 3 ins in his stockings and Henderson is reported to have lost. So it is clear that all of the other members were less than 6 ft 1 in tall.

In a roundabout way, this led to a much grander and more informative series of bets which started in 1910 when the right side of the table bet the left, including Mr Gregson, that they weighed more. The chairman was not included.

Right	Weight	Left	Weight
Weddell	10st 5 lb	Willoby	12 st 1 lb
Tiffen	13 st 4 lb	T. Fraser	12 st 3 lb
Herriot	14 st 11½ lb	Askew	14 st 4 lb
Smythe	12 st 1½ lb	C. Fraser	12 st 6 ½ lb
Griffith-Jones	11st 8 lb	Parker	13 st 2 lb
Carr	13 st	Bolam	13 st 1 lb
Darling	11 st 4 lb	Gregson	11 st 9 lb
Total	86 st 6 lb		88 st 12 ½ lb
Average	12 st 4 lbs		12 st 9 lb

This became a standard bet until the members grew bored with it and decided formally to abandon it at their meeting in 1928. But the modern generation, conscious of the passage of exactly one century, decided to view the comparison in 2010:

Right	Weight (in stone)	Left	Weight (in stone)
Crosbie Dawson	16½	Wailes-Fairbairn	13
Grounds	19½	Jeffreys	18
Landale	16¼	McKie	14½
Orpwood	14	Pardoe	14½
Joicey	15	Trotter	13
Herriot	12	Fairfax	17¾
Lovett	12¾	Douglas-Home	13¾
Farr	13	Barber	13
Totals	119		117½
Average	14^{6/7}		14½

The chairman, who was excluded from the weigh-in, was 14½ stone.

Height was not formally measured, but at least six members were over 6 ft, whilst the tallest (Grounds) was 6 ft 4 in.

The Russo-Japanese war was the subject of many wagers in between 1904 and 1906. For example, on 15 February 1904 at least eight bets were made about the likelihood of peace, the fall of Port Arthur, who would win the first land engagement, how far the conflict would spread, the number of prisoners that would be taken and the number of ships afloat or sunk. It was all speculation, but the interesting thing is that information was being fed to the wider world with fluency and detail. Today it is hard for us to remember that this was the first great conflict of the twentieth century, which proved to be possibly the most warlike 100 years the world had ever seen.

On 15 February Dr Charles Fraser bet Mr Joseph Tiffen that the commander of Russia's Baltic fleet would not have a naval engagement with the Japanese fleet by 5 February 1906. Dr Fraser could not have been more wrong. Admiral Rozhdestvenky's fleet was sighted by Japanese scouts in Tsushima Straits on 27 May and on the following day it was broken up and defeated. Russia had twenty-one vessels sunk, five captured, and only nine escaped.

With greater prescience Dr Tom Fraser bet Mr Henry Parker that peace would have been declared between Japan and Russia by 5 February 1906. Mr Parker lost because a treaty was signed on 5 September, brought about chiefly by the intervention of President Roosevelt.

This extract is taken from an article written by Anita Newcomb McGee (1864–1940) for the US National Museum of Health and Medicine:

> The Russo-Japanese War was a clash between two expanding empires. In some ways it was a very twentieth-century war, with large armies using automatic weapons; in other ways it reflected the values of the nineteenth century, with Russian citizens donating money to the Japanese Red Cross in appreciation for the care of their soldiers. Both Japan and Russia desired to enlarge their power and influence in countries that China had controlled. Previously, Japan had defeated China in the Sino-Japanese War of 1894. The Treaty of Shimonoseki ending this war gave Korea nominal independence, although Japanese settled there and controlled the railroad. Japan received Port Arthur (Lüshun) and the entire Liaodong peninsula, and thus could control the Yellow Sea. International pressure, including Russian, forced Japan to return China's territory. In 1898, Russia leased the peninsula and the ice-free harbour at Port Arthur

from the Chinese. Russia built a naval base at Port Arthur and a commercial port at Dalny (Darien). On February 8, 1904, Japan launched a surprise naval attack on Port Arthur. Japan bottled the Russian fleet in the harbour, but failed to take the port. In March, Japan's First Army occupied Korea, landing at Chemulpo (Inchon) and Nampo, and driving north for the Yalu River. In May, Japan landed more armies on the Liaodong peninsula and pushed northward, cutting off Port Arthur from reinforcements. Russia lost battles at Fuhsien and Liaoyang in the summer, but began receiving troops over the Trans-Siberian Railroad and counterattacked in the fall. Japan was becoming over-extended, yet on Jan. 2, 1905 the commander of Port Arthur surrendered.

From late February through early March, the two forces committed over one-half million men at the battle of Mukden with both suffering heavy casualties. Russia lost almost 90,000 men and the Japanese over 50,000 and perhaps up to 70,000. Mukden, the last major land battle of the war, was followed by the decisive naval Battle of Tsushima in May 1905. The Russian Baltic Fleet was attempting to reach Vladivostok in Siberia when the Japanese destroyed it. By then both sides were facing internal difficulties, financial in Japan and political in Russia, and agreed to peace negotiations led by President Theodore Roosevelt. The Treaty of Portsmouth (New Hampshire) required Russia to remove its troops from Manchuria while permitting the Japanese to hold the Liaodong peninsula and Korea. As a result of public outcry over Russian concessions in the treaty, the Czar was forced to liberalize his government, while Japan's successful military gained increasing political power.

Back at home, Captain Francis Norman bet Mr Robert Weddell that the Treasury would not allow the acceptance of Messrs Reid and Waring's present scheme for the widening of the old bridge. Fortunately, if unusually, Captain Norman won. The Treasury did not exactly condemn the plans, but declined to grant any money – and the bridge has never been enlarged.

One of the biggest scandals in the history of Berwick was alluded to by Captain John Carr, who bet Captain Orde on 15 February 1906 that Thomas Duguid would be convicted of the charge concerning the Chetwynd children. Captain Orde lost the bet.

Christopher John Leyland of Haggerston and his second wife, Helen Dora Cayley, had become the formal guardians of Mary and Amelia Chetwynd after the divorce of their parents. Mrs Chetwynd moved to Paris where she instigated a plan to have her children kidnapped from Haggerston and smuggled from Beal by sea to San Sebastian in Spain, where she intended to meet them.

A Mr Duguid and a Miss Quayle were infiltrated into the household, posing as servants. They were instructed by Mrs Chetwynd to befriend her children and members of the staff. She did not count the German Fraulein as a threat because she believed her to be a secret drinker who regularly got 'blind drunk in her bedroom'.

Although Duguid was paid handsomely to carry out the kidnapping plot, his romantic advances to Mrs Clay, the housekeeper, backfired; she cottoned on to his little scheme and shopped him. Legal proceedings dragged on from November 1905 until April 1906, when a sentence of nine months' imprisonment and a fine of £100 was passed upon Duguid. Miss Quayle was acquitted.

Leyland had enjoyed a career in both the Royal and the merchant navies before he moved to Haggerston. In the words of his great grandson, his family had done OK in Liverpool by shipping jazz musicians from one side of the Atlantic to the other. Leyland was a friend of Charles Parsons, and helped him to finance and then skipper *Turbinia*, the test vessel which Parsons built to show off his new invention, the steam turbine.

It is amusing to note part of Helen Dora's background, for she was related to Sir George Cayley, who was an inventor. One of his more enterprising schemes was to create a glider, into which he put one of his footmen – a very brave man – who was then launched from the roof of the house. History does not record the full result, although it is understood that the footman survived and Sir George gave up developing gliders.

At the meeting of the Salmon Club at the Kings Arms Hotel on 5 February 1909 there were present Mr Bolam as president, Dr C. L. Fraser, Mr F. Henderson, Mr Herriot, Mr Tiffen, Mr Weatherhead and Mr A. Weddell. Mr Darling and Mr Griffith-Jones apologised in advance for their absence.

The death which had taken place after a short illness was reported of Mr Weddell, the father of the club, having been elected in 1869 and having been the secretary since 1885, following Mr James Carl Weddell who had acted in a similar capacity. It was agreed out of respect to the memory of their oldest member to abandon the dinner for this year.

Mr Arthur Weddell was elected honorary secretary in place of his father.

On the motion of Dr C. Fraser, seconded by Mr Gregson, Mr David Hugh Watson Askew of Castle Hills was unanimously elected a member of the club.

On the night of Wednesday 15 February 1911 Mr Joseph Tiffen bet Mr Arthur Weddell that at least three of the Houndsditch prisoners would be convicted of murder, or as accessories before or after the fact. Mr Tiffen lost. The three male prisoners were acquitted; the female was convicted but then released on appeal.

This event relates to the famous Sidney Street siege. The East End of London was a hotbed of revolutionary activity, as thousands of Russian exiles found refuge there from the Czarist pogroms and Cossack reprisals after the 1905 uprising. Pre-Russian revolution assassinations, bombings and robberies were planned in London by the likes of Lenin and Stalin, when the young Winston Churchill was home secretary.

In January 1909 a wages snatch in Tottenham turned into a six-mile chase to Epping Forest, in which a policeman, a boy and the two robbers were killed by gunfire. In December 1910 a Latvian anarchist group attempted to rob a jeweller's shop in Houndsditch. As they made their getaway three policemen and one robber were shot dead, precipitating a police search of East End lodging-houses for anarchists. In January 1911 an informer landlord led police to a house in Sidney Street, Stepney, where the group's final shoot-out took place.

The Latvian anarchist Flame group were a revolutionary nationalist cell fighting the Czarist ancien regime. It consisted of Peter the Painter, Fritz Svaars, George Gardstein, Jacob Peters, Sara Trassjonsky, Nina Vassileva, Luba Milstein, Jacob Fogels, Bifsteks, Yourka Dubof, Joseph, John Rosen and Karl Hoffman. The group were also performing a revolutionary play at the Jubilee Street Anarchist Club in Stepney. As they fought the Russian revolution in London, they came up against the post-industrial power of the British Empire in the form of the City police, East End slum landlords, the young Winston Churchill and the artillery of the Scots Guards. Jacob Peters went on to be a hero of October in the 1917 revolution and one of Stalin's top men. George Gardstein, the leader of the revolutionary robbers, was shot by one of his own gang; possibly a Czarist agent-provocateur. Sara Trassjonsky, who nursed him in his last hours, was driven mad by a combination of police and anarchists. Peter the Painter disappeared and became an East End folk legend.

Looking back, it is almost incredible that there was no hint of the imminence of the First World War in the wagers laid on the night of Monday 16 February 1914. Only Mr Adam Darling had any thought about war when he bet Mr George Henderson that there would not be a mobilisation of the Ulster Volunteers on a war footing before 5 February 1915. Mr Henderson lost, but Mr Darling had been thinking not about war in Europe, but about civil war in Ireland.

The other sixty-six bets laid that night had all the flavour of a powerful country at peace. Mr John Carnaby Collingwood was attending his first dinner and accepted a wager from Mr William Bolam and Mr Frederick Griffith-Jones (described by the secretary as 'Jolam and Bones') that they would beat Mr Collingwood and Mr Carr at whist. At this time there were two Carrs in the Club: Captain John Evelyn Carr (a member from 1904–1937) and Commander Reginald Carr (1913–1927). Mr Collingwood's whist partner was probably John, who sat next to him at dinner.

Mr Carr bet Mr David Herriot that the water supply would not be pumped up to Sunnyside before 5 February 1915. In fact Mr Carr was wrong because water was pumped into Springhill Reservoir on 24 May 1914 and Shielfield Terrace was supplied on that date.

Commander Carr served on HMS *Gladiator* (5,750 tons) in 1908 under

Commander Reginald Carr, member 1913–27

Captain Walter Lumsden. During a late snowstorm off the Isle of Wight on 25 April 1908, *Gladiator* was heading into port when she struck the outbound American steamer SS *Saint Paul*. Visibility was down to 800 yards (730 m), but the strong tides and gale force winds required both ships to maintain high speeds to maintain steerage.

Lookouts on each vessel saw the approaching danger off Point Hurst. The American ship attempted to pass to the port side, the standard procedure in such a situation. Lacking room for the manoeuvre, Captain Walter Lumsden chose to turn the opposite direction, ensuring a collision. Both ships attempted to slow but both were exceptionally heavy (the *Saint Paul* was built for conversion in wartime to a cruiser). They hit at about 3 knots (5.6 km/h, or 3.5 mph). The *Saint Paul* struck *Gladiator* just aft of her engine room.

The glancing blow ripped open the sides of both ships. The British warship foundered at once, while the American ship was able to remain afloat and launch life-boats. Several men were also saved by Royal Engineers from nearby Fort Victoria. A total of twenty-seven sailors were lost, but only three bodies were recovered. *Gladiator* then settled into shallow water and was salvaged five months later. The hulk was deemed unrepairable and she was struck off the lists of duty and sold for her scrap value. A court of inquiry reprimanded Captain Lumsden in July 1908.

Colonel Pennyman was in sporting form. He bet Mr Joseph Tiffen that Tetrach would win the Derby,

Colonel Alfred Pennyman, member 1912–34

and he lost: the Derby was won by Durban II. He then bet Mr Arthur Weddell, the secretary, and Dr Charles Fraser that the Government would be out of power by 5 February 1915, losing both bets because the Government stayed in place. He won his bet against Mr David Herriot that he would beat him playing level at golf in the strawberry season. He also won his wager with Captain Frederick Allenby against Mr Edward Willoby and Commander Carr that they would win at bridge. He went on to beat Mr William Bolam in a wager that Rugby would beat Marlborough at cricket. Rugby won by five wickets.

Alfred Worsley Pennyman was of Yorkshire stock, born in 1858 with his family seat at Ormesby Hall. He served in the 25th Regiment of Foot, the King's Own Scottish Borderers, and lived outside Berwick at Ord Cottage. A search through the archives reveals why his middle name was Worsley. On 18 April 1853 in a move to ensure an inheritance, a royal licence was granted to J. W. Worsley to change his name to Pennyman and bear the arms of Pennyman. The licence was signed by Lord Palmerston and Queen Victoria.

When Mr David Herriot bet Mr Joseph Tiffen that NE consols would touch £135 he was following a traditional bet that was first laid in 1849 when Mr Thomas Cockburn bet Mr Andrew Mallock that the £3 per cent consols would not be as high as 94¾ on the last known quotation before the dinner of 1850. On this occasion, Herriot's bet was the forty-fourth in the sequence, and he lost because they only achieved £133.

Consols (originally short for consolidated annuities, but the term can now be taken to mean consolidated stock) are a form of British government bond (gilt), dating originally from the eighteenth century. They are one of the rare examples of an actual perpetuity: although they may be redeemed by the British government, they are unlikely to be redeemed in the foreseeable future. In 1752, the chancellor of the exchequer and prime minister Sir Henry Pelham converted all outstanding issues of redeemable government stock into one bond, Consolidated 3.5% annuities, in order to reduce the coupon rate paid on the government debt.

5

1920–1939

The total number of military and civilian casualties in the First World War was around 37.5 million. There were 16.5 million deaths and 21 million wounded, making it the sixth deadliest conflict in human history.

The total number of deaths includes 9.7 million military personnel and about 6.8 million civilians. The Allies lost about 5.7 million soldiers while the Central Powers lost about 4 million.

Unbelievably, no member of the Berwick Salmon Club died as the result of the war. This becomes clear from the notes of the meeting held in the Kings Arms Hotel, Berwick, on Wednesday 21 January 1920. Present were:

Mr Willoby in the chair
Mr Bolam
Mr Darling
Dr Fraser
Mr Gregson
Mr Tiffen.

Vacancies were reported in the membership owing to the deaths of Mr Weatherhead (23 February 1914) and Mr Herriot (1919), and the resignation of Mr Askew.

It was proposed by Dr Fraser and seconded by Mr Bolam that Lord Francis Godolphin Osborne, Major James Allan Herriot and Maurice Airth Coates of The Mead, Beal be elected to fill the vacancies, and the same were unanimously elected.

It was agreed to hold the annual meeting of the club on Monday 16 February in the Kings Arms Hotel, and the necessary arrangements were made with Mr Scott, the manager. Dinner would be 6/6 per head (genuinely cheap: this equates to about £7 at today's prices), champagne £1 per bottle and the port 1900 vintage.

The members who had seen war in the front line were Captain John Collingwood and Major James Herriot. Major James Herriot joined the 5th Northumberland Fusiliers in 1914 and served in the trenches in France, ultimately becoming a major and the commandant of the Lewis Machine Gun School in Le Touquet.

Sadly no record exists of the wagers taken at the dinner on 16 February 1920, although seventy-six were made by the sixteen members who attended.

After dinner on 15 February 1921 the members drank the landlord's recommended 'Royal Port', which did not satisfy them at all; it was hotly debated at the subsequent business meeting in February 1922. But this did not interfere with the wagers, some of which add real spice to the history of the times.

Mr Weddell bet Mr Tiffen that Archdeacon Wakeford would win his appeal. Weddell lost.

The Venerable John Wakeford was the archdeacon of Stow. He was commonly described as 'difficult'. Chief amongst his detractors was his brother-in-law, the Rev. Herbert Worthington, rector of Netherseal, who believed that Wakeford was treating his wife, Worthington's sister, badly. Worthington was further disenchanted by the treatment of his close hunting friend, the Rev. C. T. Moore, who had been hauled in front of a consistory court in 1915 for immoral conduct. Moore was acquitted but he and Worthington always harboured the conviction that Wakeford was covertly responsible for the charges. The trial and publicity had led to Mrs Moore having a stroke and enduring long-term illness.

In 1920, the archdeacon himself was charged with immorality. It was a huge public embarrassment, reported even by the *New York Times* on 27 April 1921. Wakeford, described by the paper as one of the most eloquent preachers in the North of England, was found guilty by the Judicial Committee of the Privy Council of misconduct on two occasions with a woman in an obscure hotel, the Bull, in Peterborough. The Judicial Committee sat as the court of appeal to review the judgement of an earlier ecclesiastical court which had also found him guilty. The archdeacon's defence was that the charges were a conspiracy by his brother-in-law, Worthington, and his friend Moore.

Many witnesses took the stand, including Mrs Wakeford, who supported her husband stoically throughout and assumed the blame for the long-standing feud between her brother and her husband. The verdict appeared to stand or fall on a chambermaid's evidence of whether the archdeacon was wearing pyjamas or a nightgown. Despite his assertion that he had never worn pyjamas, Wakeford lost his appeal and died soon afterwards.

Captain J. E. Carr bet Mr Weddell that the VC candidate would win the Woolwich election. Captain Carr won, since Captain Gee, VC, beat Ramsay Macdonald by 683 votes.

Captain Robert Gee, VC, MC (7 May 1876–2 August 1960) was born in Leicester. He was a temporary captain in the 2nd Battalion, the Royal Fusiliers during the First World War. He was awarded the Victoria Cross for his actions on 30 November 1917 at Masnières and Les Rues Vertes, France.

An attack by the enemy captured brigade headquarters and an ammunition dump. Captain Gee, finding himself a prisoner, managed to escape and organised a party of the brigade staff with which he attacked the enemy, closely followed by two companies of infantry. He cleared the locality and established a defensive flank, then finding an enemy machine-gun still in action, with a revolver in each hand he went forward and captured the gun, killing eight of the crew. He was wounded, but would not have his wound dressed until the defence was organised.

On Thursday 11 November 1920 he was one of 74 VCs serving in the honour guard for the interment of the unknown soldier in Westminster Abbey. In October of that year the dean of Westminster suggested to Buckingham Palace that the body of an unidentified soldier be exhumed from the battlefields and reburied in Westminster Abbey. To ensure the chosen warrior's identity remained unknown, the military authorities on the old Western Front were instructed to exhume six unidentified 'British' soldiers.

On 9 November 1920, six working parties commanded by subalterns went to the six main battlefields – Aisne, Arras, Cambrai, Marne, Somme and Ypres – each to exhume the remains of one soldier buried in a grave marked 'unknown'. The six bodies were put in coffins and taken to a hut near Ypres where they were received by a clergyman. A blindfolded officer went inside the hut and at random touched the coffin of the soldier who was to be laid among kings in Westminster Abbey. The body was brought across the English Channel from Boulogne to Dover on HMS *Verdun*. Following a brief service the unknown warrior was lowered into his grave near the Great West Door on 11 November 1920. The grave was refilled with earth brought from the battlefields.

Gee first stood for Parliament as a National Democratic Party candidate in the 1918 General Election at Consett, where he finished second. He then stood as a Conservative in the 1921 Woolwich East by-election against Ramsay MacDonald. A great deal of attention was given in the campaign to the contrast between Gee as a VC holder and MacDonald as a pacifist who had opposed the war. Gee won the seat.

He died in Perth, Australia, aged eighty-four. He was cremated at the Karrakatta crematorium. His VC is displayed at the Royal Fusiliers Museum in the Tower of London, England.

Local affairs were enshrined in two wagers. First, Captain John Carr bet Mr Joseph Tiffen that no house in the Tweedmouth Housing Scheme would be occupied on or before 2 August. Captain Carr won, since Oliver, the first occupier, entered on 6 September.

Dr Charles Fraser bet Captain John Collingwood that the takings at the ladies lavatory would exceed 200 pence. Dr Fraser won because more than 1,000 ladies made use of the facility.

At the 1922 dinner Captain Carr bet Mr George Henderson that Eamonn de Valera would be shot before 5 February 1923. Captain Carr lost.

De Valera played a key role in Ireland's history. He was one of the leaders in the 1916 Easter Uprising. He was also president of Sinn Fein from 1917 to 1926 and became taoiseach for much of the 1950s, then subsequently president of an independent Ireland. Born in 1882 in New York, his mother was Irish and his father was Spanish. Though de Valera was born in America, he was educated in Ireland and became a mathematics lecturer at Maynooth.

The uprising failed and the seven leaders were executed, along with nine other rebels. De Valera was sentenced to death as an organiser of the revolt but was to escape the firing squad because of the confusion surrounding his ancestry (the English authorities did not want to risk the execution of an American citizen). Nevertheless, he continued to resist the rule of London, so was arrested and sent to Lincoln prison. He escaped from jail in 1919 and went to America. Here he spent a year and a half touring the country in an attempt to raise money for Sinn Fein. His efforts were very successful and he raised over £1 million for the cause. A lot of this money went into the newly formed Irish Republican Army (IRA – formed in January 1919). He retired from politics aged ninety in 1973 and died in 1975.

Lord Francis Osborne bet Captain Carr that Princess Mary would not have a baby before 5 February 1923. Lord Francis won narrowly by two days, since a son was born at 11.15 pm on 7 February.

Princess Mary was the third child and only daughter of George V and Queen Mary. She married Henry, Viscount Lascelles, son of the fifth earl of Harewood, on 28 February 1922, and gave birth to their first son, George, who became the seventh earl.

Lord Francis Osborne bet Mr James Darling that subscriptions to the Berwick war memorial would reach £2,500 by 5 February 1923. Disappointingly, Mr Osborne lost because subscriptions amounted to just over £2,100. This was followed in 1923 by Captain John Carr betting Mr Joseph

Tiffen that the Berwick war memorial would not be completed before 5 February 1924. Mr Carr lost: the memorial was unveiled by Earl Haig on 11 November 1923.

Mr Arthur Weddell, who did not attend the dinner, bet Dr Charles Fraser that foot and mouth disease would be stamped out before 5 February 1923. Mr Weddell was wrong.

Modern readers will certainly be aware of the 2001 and 2007 outbreaks of foot and mouth disease in the United Kingdom, and some may well remember the 1967 outbreak. So it comes as something of a shock that it was a major issue back in 1923, and Mr Weddell's belief that it would be stamped out within the year has proven to be something of a pipe dream.

In fact the disease has probably been a scourge ever since bovines were first gathered in herds. In 1897 Friedrich Loeffler demonstrated that it was viral. The USA has had nine outbreaks since 1870. The most devastating one happened in 1914 and originated in Michigan. About 3,500 livestock herds were infected across the USA, totalling over 170,000 cattle, sheep and swine.

Dr Thomas Caverhill bet Captain John Carr that another lot of houses under the Tweedmouth housing scheme would be started before 5 February 1923. Dr Caverhill won because twenty-four were started in March 1922.

A year later Captain Carr bet the Rev. W. M. Smythe that someone would be injured through a collision of charabancs on the Old Bridge before 5 February 1924. This bet was lost by Mr Carr. A lady was killed by a motor lorry, but no accident occurred owing to a collision of charabancs.

Commander Reginald Carr bet Dr Charles Fraser that the mummy of Tutankhamen would not be found in the tomb at Luxor before 5 February 1924. Commander Carr won.

The Earl of Caernarvon financed Howard Carter's excavations at Luxor from 1914. The war interrupted the work until 1917 when it was resumed in earnest. But after a time, Caernarvon became disillusioned and in 1922 gave Carter notice that he would fund only one more year.

On 4 November 1922, Carter's water carrier found the steps leading to Tutankhamen's tomb, by far the best preserved and most intact pharaonic tomb ever found in the Valley of the Kings. He wired Caernarvon to come, and on 26 November 1922, with Caernarvon, Caernarvon's daughter, and others in attendance, Carter made the famous 'tiny breach in the top left-hand corner' of the doorway, and was able to peer in by the light of a candle to see that many of the gold and ebony treasures were still in place.

There followed several months of laborious cataloguing before Carter opened a sealed doorway on 16 February 1923. It led to a burial chamber, with a sarcophagus which proved to be that of Tutankhamen.

After the 1924 dinner Captain Frederick Allenby bet Mr Delaval Gregson that the new bridge across the Tweed at Berwick would be started before 5 February 1925. Captain Allenby won, since Holloway Bros started building in January 1925.

The Royal Tweed Bridge was designed by L. G. Mouchel & Partners and built by Holloway Bros Ltd between 1924 and 1928. The bridge cost a total of £180,000 and up to 170 people were employed in its construction. As early as 1896 a new road bridge had been planned for the site to carry the A1 road from London to Edinburgh across the River Tweed, as a means of diverting traffic from the adjacent seventeenth-century Old Bridge. When built, the bridge possessed the longest reinforced concrete arch in Britain and was also the country's longest highway viaduct.

Captain Frederick Allenby, member 1913–32

The bridge was opened with great ceremony by the prince of Wales, later King Edward VIII, on 16 May 1928.

Captain Allenby enjoyed his first dinner with the club in 1913. He resigned in 1932, although he missed the dinner in 1930. He was awarded a CBE in 1919 and served as a JP. Born on 21 September 1864, he died on 1 August 1934. His brother was Field Marshal Viscount Allenby of Megiddo (1861–1936), who had no children, so Captain Allenby's son Dudley became the second Viscount Allenby.

In 1926 Mr Joseph Tiffen bet Captain John Collingwood that the duchess of York would have a daughter before 5 February 1927. Tiffen was right: a daughter, Elizabeth Alexandra Mary, was born on 21 April 1926.

As this book goes to print, that daughter has been on the throne of England for sixty years, having succeeded

Captain Jack Briggs, member 1924–47, and his son Johnny

her father on 6 February 1952. Elizabeth II is the constitutional monarch of sixteen sovereign states known as the Commonwealth realms: the United Kingdom, Canada, Australia, New Zealand, Jamaica, Barbados, the Bahamas, Grenada, Papua New Guinea, the Solomon Islands, Tuvalu, Saint Lucia, Saint Vincent and the Grenadines, Belize, Antigua and Barbuda, and Saint Kitts and Nevis. As head of the Commonwealth, she is the figurehead of the fifty-four-member Commonwealth of Nations and is the titular head of a quarter of the world's population; as the British monarch, she is the Supreme Governor of the Church of England.

Captain Allenby bet Captain Jack Briggs that he would get more wild duck between 1 August 1926 and 5 February 1927 than last season. Captain Allenby lost. Captain Briggs created a post-war record of fifty-two duck (forty-eight picked up) in one shoot, but the total was less than the previous season.

Captain Briggs was born on 24 October 1896 and was commissioned into the Durham Light Infantry in 1914. Subsequently he was posted to the 6th Battalion the Machine Gun Corps. He was mentioned in despatches (*London Gazette* 28 December 1918) and awarded a Military Cross (*London Gazette* 3 January 1919) for his service in France during the Great War. Both he and his brother Scott were good horsemen, but Jack was much better known and respected as a brilliant shot. He married Nora Carnaby Collingwood, daughter of John Collingwood of Cornhill, in 1921 and they had a son, John Leonard Collingwood Briggs, who was born on 26 April 1923. Poor Captain Briggs was to face two major tragedies. Nora died on 15 June 1936 at the age of thirty-three. The death certificate shows that the cause was acute alcoholism. And their son was shot dead by a German sniper in the final hours of the war on 15 April 1945 outside Celle, near Hanover in Germany. There was another cruel coincidence about the date and place. Celle is less than 15 miles from the site of Belsen concentration camp, which was liberated the same day. Captain Briggs never attended the meetings of the club again after 1939, although he did not resign until 1947. He died in 1976.

In 1927 Mr Maurice Coates bet Mr Joseph Tiffen that the new theatre would be opened for entertainment before the next dinner. Mr Coates lost. The theatre was opened by Captain Allenby on 2 July 1928, and the first picture to be shown was *The Flag Lieutenant.*

Captain Christopher Leyland, member in 1927

This was the only year in which Mr Christopher Digby Leyland attended the dinner. He was elected at the business meeting on 5 February 1926 to fill the vacancy caused by the death of Lord Francis Osborne, and resigned in 1931. Also elected that night was Mr Digby Cayley. Mr Leyland's grandson has provided a marvellous insight into his grandfather: 'Christopher Digby was not the calibre of his father but he had a "fine leg for a boot". Horses and women were his passion. Unfortunately the women tended to be faster than the horses.' In the First World War he saw action in the Middle East and the trenches. Between the wars, he was, like many of the wealthy survivors, reluctant to accept that things had changed. He sold Haggerston and the sporting estate of Kidland Lea along with the few thousand acres attached. He moved to Camp Hill near Wetherby and then to Porlock in Somerset.

At Porlock he and a friend set up a riding school for 'nice girls and boys'. He had a son and two daughters by his first wife, a Cottrell from Herefordshire. That marriage failed when she ran off with his pet jockey. Mr Leyland had lent the man his London flat to recuperate after a tumble over the fences, and Granny Leyland cleared off to mop his brow. His second wife was Enid, later to become Enid Goodson. His third wife was Violet, who proved to be a terrifying step-grandmother.

During the Second World War, Mr Leyland volunteered as a mounted policeman in London, taking his own horses with him in order to ensure that they were not requisitioned by the army. He died in 1970.

In 1928 Mr Joseph Tiffen bet Captain Donald Gibsone that someone would be hanged for the Pembridge Square murder. Mr Tiffen was absolutely right.

On Thursday 9 February 1928, Alfred Webb was shot dead in Flat 3, 20 Pembridge Square, Notting Hill. One Frederick Stewart, aged twenty-eight, was quickly arrested and appeared before Mr Justice Avory at the Old Bailey on 18 April. He was found guilty and sentenced to hang at Pentonville Prison on Wednesday 6 June 1928. The hangman was Robert Baxter, and his assistant Thomas Phillips (information taken from British Executions website, http://britishexecutions.co.uk/execution-content. php?key=496&time=1314232276).

1929 saw Mr David Herriot bet Mr James Herriot that Malcolm Campbell would establish a new mile speed record. Mr David lost. Campbell got the five-mile record at 212 mph, but Henry Seagrave did over 231 mph for a mile.

Campbell broke the land speed record for the first time in 1924, clocking 146.16 mph at Pendine Sands near Carmarthen Bay in a 350HP V12 Sunbeam. He broke nine land speed records between 1924 and 1935, with three at Pendine Sands and five at Daytona Beach. His first two records were driving a racing car manufactured by the Sunbeam Car Company in Wolverhampton.

On 4 February 1927 Campbell set the world land speed record at Pendine Sands covering the flying kilometre in a mean average of 174.883 mph and the flying mile in 174.224 mph in the Napier-Campbell *Blue Bird*. He set his final land speed record at the Bonneville Salt Flats in Utah on 3 September 1935, and was the first person to drive an automobile over 300 miles per hour (301.337 mph).

His son Donald went on to emulate his father's performance on land and water by setting seven world speed records on water (a feat still unparalleled). Indeed, he remains the only person ever to have set both land and water world records in the same year. Sadly he died on Coniston Water on 4 January 1967 when his boat, *Bluebird K7*, flipped and disintegrated when travelling at over 300 mph.

Captain John Carr bet Mr Claude Darling that Smith would beat Lindrum in Australia. Captain Carr won.

Sidney Smith and Horace Lindrum were leading billiards players in the 1920s and 1930s, but had the misfortune of facing Joe Davis, who was world champion from 1927 to 1940, then again after the war in 1946. Lindrum was runner-up in 1936 and 1937 and actually won in 1952. Smith was runner-up in 1938 and 1939.

Mr Maurice Coates, who was a member of the club from 1920 to 1935, evidently had some expectation that he would get married to 'a widow' during the following year. Not only did he bet Mr James Darling that he would be married to her before 5 February 1930, but Mr James Herriot, Captain John Collingwood and Captain Frederick Allenby all bet Coates that he would not be 'churched'. Poor chap – he lost every bet.

The range of wagers in 1930 was traditional, but there was clearly a lack of weighty material for the members to use. This led to some very light-hearted banter.

Dr Thomas Caverhill bet Mr Claude Darling that there are an odd number of tulips on the table. This was lost by Dr Caverhill. Mr Digby Cayley laid the same bet with Captain Allenby and also lost.

Commander Hugh Lillingston, attending his first dinner, bet Mr James Herriot that he would blow a hen's egg from one glass to another in three blows. This was lost by Commander Lillingston, who succeeded on the fifth attempt. As a side bet, Mr Darling successfully bet Commander Lillingston that he would break the egg.

On high form but with poor judgement, Commander Lillingston then bet Captain John Carr that he had an even number of coins in his pocket, and lost.

Captain Allenby then bet Mr George Henderson, who was not present at the dinner, that he would not ride a scooter down Hide Hill from Miss Farr's to Sandgate. Not surprisingly, Mr Henderson lost.

In 1931 we see the first signs of the Spanish Civil War, when Mr George Henderson, who did not attend a dinner after 1928 until he resigned in

1933, bet Captain Frederick Allenby that King Alfonso would abdicate the throne of Spain. Mr Henderson lost, even though Alfonso left Spain on 14 April 1931, because he did not abdicate.

Always at home with rural affairs, members often laid bets about the behaviour of animals. On this occasion, Colonel Gerald Leather, attending his only dinner, bet Mr William Bolam that a heron does not take 150 flaps to a minute. Mr Bolam lost, since observation showed the rate was 130–140 flaps per minute.

At dinner on 15 February 1932, Mr Digby Cayley was fined one bottle of wine for smoking before the toast to the King and Queen. Fines were not a normal ingredient of the club's affairs, although Dr Samuel Edgar was fined in 1842 for 'breach of privilege' for having altered a bet taken down by the honorary secretary without the permission of the chairman or the company; the alteration being the obliteration of the word 'not' in the substantive part of the original of the first bet made that evening. Mr Henry Short was also fined in 1842 for having left the room for two hours without the consent of the chairman. Thereafter the subject of fines never arose until Lt Col Tom Fairfax suggested the institution of a fines book at the business meeting in November 2010. A decision was held over until the business meeting in November 2011, when the notion of fines was laid to rest.

Captain Alan Goodson was elected at the business meeting on 8 February 1932 to replace the ephemeral Colonel Gerald Leather. At his first dinner that year, he bet Captain John Collingwood that he could not think of two words with three consecutive 's's in them. Captain Goodson lost, since Captain Collingwood immediately suggested Inverness-shire and Ross-shire.

One year later Captain John Carr bet Mr James Herriot that the £3,000 required for the renovations of Berwick Parish Church would have been subscribed by 5 February 1934 if a national appeal were made. Captain Carr won. About £3,500 was given or promised, but by that time the appeal organisers had realised that a total of £4,500 (some £162,000 in 2010 terms) was required. It must be said that this sort of poor planning remains common with charities today.

Captain Carr continued his evening by betting Mr Digby Cayley that there would be war between China and Japan. Captain Carr's instincts were good, according to the formal records, but the fact is that he should have lost because the incursion by Japan in 1933 did not escalate to war.

In 1931 the situation in China provided an easy opportunity for Japan to further its goals. It saw Manchuria as a limitless supply of raw materials, a market for its manufactured goods and as a protective buffer state against the Soviet Union in Siberia. Militarily too weak to directly challenge Japan, China appealed to the League of Nations for help. The League's investigation was published as the Lytton Report, condemning Japan for its incursion into Manchuria, and causing Japan to withdraw from the League of Nations entirely. Appeasement being the predominant policy of the day, no country was willing to take action against Japan beyond tepid censure.

In 1933, the Japanese attacked the Great Wall region, leading to the Tanggu Truce, which gave Japan control of Rehe province as well as a demilitarised zone between the Great Wall and Beiping-Tianjin region. This formally ended the invasion of Manchuria.

With the benefit of hindsight, it is uncomfortable to look back at the bet made on the night of 15 February 1933 by Commander Hugh Lillingston against Mr James Herriot (and against Captain Alan Goodson in a second, duplicate bet) that Hitler would not be German Chancellor on 5 February 1934. Commander Lillingston could never have foreseen what was about to happen.

Hitler was sworn in as German chancellor by the most reluctant president, Paul von Hindenburg, on 30 January 1933. Franz von Papen was vice-chancellor. Hindenburg had promised him that Hitler would only be received in the office of the president if accompanied by Papen. This was another way to keep Hitler in check. In fact, Papen had every intention of using the conservative majority in the cabinet along with his own political skills to run the government himself.

'Within two months we will have pushed Hitler so far in the corner that he'll squeak,' Papen boasted to a political colleague.

Papen and many non-Nazis thought having Hitler as chancellor was to their advantage. Conservative members of the former aristocratic ruling class desired an end to the republic and a return to an authoritarian government that would restore Germany to glory and bring back their old privileges. They wanted to go back to the days of the Kaiser. For them, putting Hitler in power was just the first step toward achieving that goal. They knew it was likely he would wreck the republic. Then once the republic was abolished, they could put in someone of their own choosing, perhaps even a descendant of the Kaiser.

Big bankers and industrialists, including Alfred Krupp and I. G. Farben, had lobbied Hindenburg and schemed behind the scenes on behalf of Hitler because they were convinced he would be good for business. He promised to be for free enterprise and keep down communism and the trade union movements.

The military also placed its bets on Hitler, believing his repeated promises to tear up the Treaty of Versailles and expand the army to bring back its former glory.

These factions all had one thing in common – they underestimated Hitler.

Meanwhile, an old comrade of Hitler's sent a telegram to President Hindenburg regarding his new chancellor. Former General Erich Ludendorff had once supported Hitler and had even participated in the failed Beer Hall Putsch in 1923. His telegram said:

> By appointing Hitler Chancellor of the Reich you have handed over our sacred German Fatherland to one of the greatest demagogues of all time. I prophesy to you this evil man will plunge our Reich into the abyss and will inflict immeasurable woe on our nation. Future generations will curse you in your grave for this action.

Within weeks, Hitler would be absolute dictator of Germany and would set in motion a chain of events resulting in the Second World War and the eventual deaths of nearly 50 million humans through that war and through deliberate extermination.

That same evening, Mr David Herriot bet Mr Maurice Coates that there would be no legislation against 'bodyline' bowling passed before 5 February 1934 by the MCC. Mr Herriot won.

The arrival of the English touring side in Australia for the Ashes series during the summer of 1932–1933 was much anticipated by all Australian cricket fans. The English captain, Douglas Jardine, was about to write his team into the record and history books for all the wrong reasons. To counter the skill of the great Australian player Donald Bradman, who had devastated the English bowling attack during the 1930 series, Jardine adopted a tactic later to become known as bodyline.

This involved the placing of a least five players close in to the batsman, and the bowler continually bowling a barrage of short-pitched balls aimed at leg stump. These balls would quickly rear up from the pitch, placing the batsman in danger of serious injury. To counter these rising deliveries, the batsman was forced to adopt defensive batting strokes, which would regularly result in catches to the close-in fielders.

Bradman, an exceptionally gifted and attacking batsman, was affected by the close-in fielders, who interfered with his concentration. In the second test held in Melbourne, Bradman was dismissed by English bowler Bill Bowes without scoring. Many Australian players were subsequently injured as a result of the bodyline tactics. It was not only the Australian players who were aghast at the despicable tactics of the English, but also the Australian cricket authorities.

The Australian Cricket Board sent an urgent telegram to its counterpart in England demanding they instruct Jardine to discontinue his methods. For the sake of cricket and sportsmanship the Australians pleaded with the English to refrain. Discussions were even held in the Australian Parliament to find a way to stop the Englishmen from devastating and tarnishing the game of cricket.

High-level diplomatic meetings were held between the English and the Australians, and eventually Jardine was ordered to refrain from his dangerous tactics. The Englishmen eventually went on to win back the Ashes from Australia: bodyline had served their purpose. They had contained and restrained the great Donald Bradman.

Although the MCC failed to take firm action before 5 February 1934, the laws of cricket were changed eventually to ensure that the spirit of the game was protected.

Despite the tremors shaking Europe with the advent of Adolf Hitler, the members of the Berwick Salmon Club were almost entirely engaged with sporting and home affairs after dinner the whole way through the period from 1934 to 1939. Out of 401 bets, there were no more than six references to the evolution of fascism and the possibility of war. Indeed, it is almost as if the club (and maybe the nation?) was shuffling towards the Second World War with its eyes closed.

Mr Digby Cayley bet Mr Joseph Tiffen that no Englishman would report seeing the Loch Ness monster. This was lost by Mr Cayley, because Mr C. Watt of Armstrong Whitworth & Co Ltd, Newcastle, reported seeing the monster on Easter Monday 1934.

Lt Col John Sale, attending his first dinner, teased fellow member Mr Percy Swan that Mr Swan could not produce anything more vulgar than his cufflinks. Lost by Mr Swan, who only attended five dinners between 1933 and 1937 but somehow remained a member of the club until he resigned in 1950.

Mr Swan bet Mr Maurice Coates that Berwick Laundry sheets were stiffer than Kelso ones. This too was lost by Mr Swan.

Mr David Herriot bet Captain Donald Gibsone that the 1935 tonnage at Berwick Harbour would be greater than 1934. Mr Herriot won. The statistics were 1934, 15,533; 1935, 19,536.

Major Ronnie Bell bet Captain John Carr that the king's engagement would be announced before 5 February 1937. This was lost by Bell, but it was a most interesting and timely bet.

The bet was laid on the night of 15 February 1936. On 16 November 1936, King Edward VIII told his prime minister, Stanley Baldwin, that he wished to marry Mrs Simpson when she was free to do so. She had the mild embarrassment of a second husband to dispose of first. The Government and the Church were totally against the idea of a divorced woman becoming queen, so Edward proposed a morganatic marriage (in which he would be king, but she would not hold the position of queen). Baldwin offered the king three alternatives: give up the idea of marrying Mrs Simpson; marry her and face the consequences (which would have been a constitutional crisis because the Government would have resigned); or abdicate. The king chose to abdicate, and duly signed the instruments of abdication at Fort Belvedere on 10 December 1936.

Major Bell was elected to the club in 1935 and resigned in 1951. Commissioned in the King's Own Scottish Borderers in 1913, he was wounded early in the First World War and taken prisoner, where he remained until 1918. He had three sons who all joined the RAF in the Second World War but only one, Peter, survived. Later he went to farm in Africa.

There was a hint of the future, when Mr Digby Cayley bet Captain John Collingwood that Great Britain would be drawn into war before 5 February 1937. Mr Cayley lost, as we know. On 15 February 1938, Commander Hugh Lillingston bet Mr David Herriot that the Fuhrer, Hitler, would no longer be in power. Commander Lillingston lost, as did Lt Col John Sale who bet Dr Vincent Badcock that Mussolini's tin shirt would be punctured by a bullet.

Dr Badcock, who joined the club in 1937 and resigned in 1950, died on 6 April 1954 at Flodden Lodge. He was awarded his Military Cross for conspicuous gallantry during the First World War by continuing to provide medical aid under fire when he was wounded. His wounds eventually meant that he had his leg amputated below the knee. He was a keen cricketer and played regularly for the Tillside Club, of which he became chairman.

Subsequently, Commander Lillingston bet Mr Herriot in February 1939 that Hitler would not be Fuhrer on 5 February 1940. Commander Lillingston lost again. Hitler was only ever mentioned once more, when Mr W. R. Sitwell bet Major Eustace Maxwell on 22 February 1952 that Hitler was alive at midnight that night. Mr Sitwell lost, of course.

After dinner in 1937, Mr Percy Swan bet Mr David Herriot that the price of petrol, currently 1/7, would go up by tuppence. The bet was lost by Mr

Dr Vincent Badcock, member 1937–50

Swan. The purchasing power of one pound in 1937 would be about £33 today, so the comparative cost of a gallon of petrol would be £2.61. The price on the pump as at 1 September 2011 was £1.35 per litre, which amounts to £6.14 per gallon, most of which is made up of duty.

On the eve of war, the members unknowingly enjoyed their final club dinner for six years. Captain John Evelyn Carr, who became a member in 1899, had resigned. Professor William Hume had been elected in his place, but he failed to attend the dinner because he was ill. The members drank Perrier Jouet 1928 and Cockburn's 1927 port, paying 2/6 corkage for the pleasure. Sir Charles Furness was in the chair, having lost nine wagers in 1938, while Captain Alan Goodson was vice-chairman, having won eight wagers the previous year. Poor Captain Goodson would never attend another dinner because he died in 1941.

Sir Charles Furness bet Commander Lillingston that there would be an inquest on a sudden death on Goswick Golf Course. Sir Charles lost, although it was curious that eighty seagulls were found frozen in a bunker at the course during the year. There was no inquest.

Dr Vincent Badcock bet Sir Charles that the vicar of Branxton would not be 'blessed' (presumably with the birth of a child). Dr Badcock won this easy wager: the vicar was ninety-four years old.

Mr Digby Cayley bet Commander Lillingston that he would sell Horncliffe House that year. The commander lost, and it was Mr Cayley who bought the house!

Captain Alan Goodson bet Mr Henry McCreath that Scott Briggs' horse, Macmoffet, would not get around the Grand National course. Captain Goodson lost, and Macmoffet came in second. And in another bet concerning the Grand National, Mr Cayley bet Captain John Collingwood that the winner of the Grand National would start at 40–1 or more. Cayley lost because the winner, Workman, was at 100–8.

Sir Charles Furness bet Captain Collingwood that the Collingwood Arms would appear in a police case. Sir Charles won because the proprietor was fined for not screening lights during black-out hours.

6
1946–1972

The meeting of the Salmon Club at the Kings Arms Hotel on 24 January 1946 was the first since 1939. Present were:

Captain Collingwood
Sir Charles Furness, Bt.
Mr D. R. Herriot
Major J. A. Herriot
Lt Col John Sale.

It was reported that four vacancies existed owing to the deaths of Captain D. H. Gibsone and Captain A. R. Goodson, and the resignation of Mr D. L. A. Cayley and Commander Lillingston. It was agreed to invite Lt Col George Horace Davidson, Lt Col Robert Allen Fenwick Thorp, Major John Home Robertson and Mr Thomas Straker-Smith to become members of the club. Mr Straker-Smith declined the invitation.

The meeting agreed that the annual dinner be held on 15 February at 7.00 pm for 7.30 pm. Arrangements were left in the hands of the secretary.

On 15 February 1946 the club met at the Kings Arms. Present were:

Mr A. W. Paton in the chair, having lost nine bets at the meeting in 1939
Dr V. E. Badcock (vice-chairman)
Major R. P. M. Bell
Captain J. C. Collingwood
Mr W. N. Crawhall
Lt Col H. Davidson
Sir Charles Furness
Mr D. R. Herriot
Major J. A. Herriot
Major J. Home Robertson
Professor W. E. Hume
Dr P. W. MacLagan
Lt Col J. W. Sale
Lt Col R. A. F. Thorp

Apologies for absence were received from Captain J. M. Briggs, Mr H. G. McCreath and Mr P. C. Swan – indeed Captain Briggs and Mr Swan never attended another dinner, while Mr McCreath attended only in 1948, 1949, 1950 and 1951 before resigning.

The war had had a terrible impact on the participants. The Soviet Union lost 29 million people (12 million military and 17 million civilian); Poland 6.27 million, the vast majority being civilian; Germany 5.69 million, and Yugoslavia 1.6 million. Great Britain had 403,000 military and 92,700 civilian deaths, whilst France lost 245,000 soldiers, sailors and airmen and 350,000 civilians. The USA, late into the war, nevertheless lost 413,000 people.

As with the First World War, no member of the club had died through enemy action.

Major Jock Home Robertson bet Lt Col Horace Davidson that all except two of the Nuremberg war criminals would be hanged. Major Home Robertson lost because just ten out of twenty-two were hanged. Goering committed suicide, and the others were imprisoned or released.

Mr Alastair Paton bet Mr James Herriot that petrol rationing would not cease before 1 October 1946. Mr Paton won.

After the outbreak of the war in September 1939, the first commodity to be controlled was petrol, but food rationing was also introduced quite early. On 8 January 1940, bacon, butter and sugar were rationed. This was followed by meat, tea, jam, biscuits, breakfast cereals, cheese, eggs, lard, milk and canned fruit. At the 1950 General Election, the Conservative Party campaigned on a manifesto of ending rationing as quickly as possible. During the following Labour-controlled parliament, petrol rationing ended on 26 May 1950.

Arrangements for the 1947 dinner were discussed at the Kings Arms Hotel on 30 January of that year. The plan was to dine on Friday 15 February, but the weather was so bad that the dinner was postponed firstly to 28 February and again to 14 March. By ill luck the same weather conditions prevailed and the dinner was abandoned for the year.

Most of the wagers in 1948 and 1949 were of a sporting nature, but Sir Charles Furness bet Captain John Collingwood in 1948 that he would commit an abortionist to prison. This was lost by Sir Charles.

Captain John Carnaby Collingwood, born on 1 October 1870, joined the Northumberland Royal Garrison Artillery at the advanced age of 44. This meant that he was never going to be front-line material. He was very much the country gentleman, the inheritor of a reasonable-sized estate who, like his father before him, enjoyed hunting, shooting and fishing in their due season. He was on the Bench for a long time and spent 25 years as Bench chairman. His colleagues clubbed together to present him with a silver salver to mark the event, possibly as a delicate hint that enough was enough. By chance the salver was eventually passed to Eric Grounds, Captain Collingwood's great-nephew through marriage, when he was Bench chairman. He inscribed it with the names of those who had been chairman in the intervening years, and it is now passed by the incumbent to his or her successor. In the modern magisterial system, no one can serve for more than three years as chairman.

On the night of 15 February 1950 Dr Vincent Badcock bet Mr John Lindsay that Winston Churchill would have a bigger majority than Clement Attlee in the General Election scheduled for the following week. Dr Badcock was right: Churchill secured 18,499 votes, and Attlee 12,107.

This wager could have been interpreted in a completely different way because Churchill was the leader of the Conservative Party, while Attlee led Labour. Here the bet would have gone Mr Lindsay's way, because Labour secured 50.4 per cent of the popular vote (13,226,176) while the Conservatives achieved only 45.12 per cent (11,507,061). Despite polling over 1.5 million votes more than the Conservatives, the election, held on 23 February 1950, resulted in Labour receiving a slim majority of just five seats over all other parties, and the party called another General Election in 1951.

Captain Collingwood bet Lt Col John Sale that there would not be more than twenty lady MPs returned at the General Election. The captain lost, since the Conservatives returned six, the Liberals one and Labour fourteen, making a total of twenty-one. Today (2011) there are 144 female MPs.

Captain Collingwood, Lt Col Horace Davidson, Mr Allan Herriot, Mr David Herriot, Lt Col George Kennedy, Dr Philip MacLagan, Mr Bill McCreath, and Mr Alastair Paton attended the business meeting in the Kings Arms Hotel on 9 February 1952. They stood in silence in memory of his late Majesty, King George VI, and unanimously agreed that the dinner would not be held on 15 February, which was the day of the late king's funeral. It was further agreed to hold it on Friday 22 February instead, at 7.00 pm for 7.30 pm.

In a flurry of bets based upon the Second World War and its consequences, Major Eustace Maxwell lost two bets and won one. He bet Major Home Robertson that hostilities would cease in Korea, and lost, because the war lasted from 25 June 1950 to 27 July 1953. This was the first significant conflict of the Cold War, a proxy war because the two principal contestants, North and South Korea, were sponsored by external powers (China and the United Nations respectively).

Mr Maxwell also lost his bet with Mr David Herriot that Stalin would be dead. Stalin died a little over twelve months later on 5 March 1953. And Mr W. R. Sitwell bet him that Hitler was alive at midnight that night. Unsurprisingly Mr Sitwell lost, since Hitler's death had been well recorded in 1945.

Over the years members have laid some extraordinarily silly bets:

The number of coins in a pocket.

The number of flowers in a vase.

The number of glasses on the table.

That a particular member would not kill six mice by hand.

That one member had more £1 notes in his pocket than his neighbour.

That the member could not count the number of Hs on a Gold Flake packet.

That a cigar would not stay alight for another fifteen minutes (it lasted twenty-five).

That a member would not windsurf in the nude.

That Glasgow is east of Bristol (Glasgow is 4°12'W, Bristol is 2°35'W). The wager was repeated the following year.

That the Kings Arms cat has kittens within a fortnight.

That nobody gets hiccups.

That there was an uneven number of chairs in the room.

That there was an even number of letters on a cigar container.

That one member had an even number of fly buttons, while the other had an odd number.

That an able-bodied member, who had to accept the bet, had four fingers and a thumb on each hand.

That the winning horses of two specific flat races would have names starting with the same letter.

That a member would not stand on one leg entirely unsupported for ten minutes. The bet would be doubled if he had the other leg draped around the back of his neck.

It was after dinner in 1953 that Lt Col George Kennedy bet Lt Col Lionel Machin that a mile would be run in four minutes or less by the next dinner. In the event, Lt Col Kennedy lost by a matter of a few weeks.

On 6 May 1954, Roger Bannister completed a mile race in Oxford in 3 minutes 59.4 seconds. His record lasted for a mere forty-six days:

Bannister's key rival, the Australian John Landy, ran the mile in 3 minutes 57.9 seconds at Turku in Finland. The fastest time ever recorded is 3 minutes 43.13 seconds, run by the Moroccan, Hicham El Guerrouj on 7 July 1999 in Rome. Lt Col Kennedy repeated this wager successfully in 1954 against Dr Philip MacLagan.

Dr MacLagan had won a Military Cross during the Great War when he was a medical officer for the Royal Northumberland Fusiliers. He was discharged from the army in 1919 and returned to Berwick to practise medicine in the community. His surgery and home was at 2 Love Lane, Bankhill, where he lived with his wife, Jane Scott Robinson. They married on 1 September 1915 and had two children, Mary (born 8 February 1918) and Philip (born 26 March 1922). Tragically, Mary drowned in the River Whiteadder in 1932, while Philip emigrated to Australia in 1960 and died two years before his father on 23 July 1973. Philip senior was awarded an OBE in the New Year's Honours list in 1959 for his services to medicine. He died on 6 May 1975,

Young Philip MacLagan married Joan Marion Herriot, the daughter of Alderman James Allan Herriot, on 22 December 1947.

Still in 1953 Mr William Gilchrist bet Mr Allan Herriot that there would be no reduction in the purchase tax on cars. He was spectacularly wrong. On 15 April 1953 the tax was reduced by 25 per cent, from $66^{2/3}$ per cent to 50 per cent.

In 1955 Mr David Herriot successfully bet Major Eustace Maxwell that Chiang Kai-Shek would still be in power in Formosa (Taiwan) at the next dinner. Chiang Kai-Shek was president from 20 May 1948 until his death on 5 April 1975, so Mr Herriot won.

The likelihood of a General Election in the United Kingdom featured in several wagers. Four years had elapsed since the last election, so it was entirely possible, even probable, that an election would be called. It was held on 26 May 1955 and resulted in an increase of sixty seats for the Conservatives. Mr Machin had bet Lt Col Davidson that Churchill would not be premier on 31 January 1956, and that was exactly what happened, because Anthony Eden took over the leadership of the Conservative Party on 7 April 1955. Interestingly, the 1955 election is the earliest for which television coverage survives.

A year later, Captain John Collingwood bet Mr Bill McCreath that Gamal Abdel Nasser would not be in power in Egypt by the next dinner (in February 1957). Captain Collingwood was wrong.

This was a particularly imaginative wager because it preceded Nasser's nationalisation of the Suez Canal Company and the resulting Suez crisis, which began on 29 October 1956 with the Israeli invasion of Sinai. Britain and France, who were major shareholders in the canal, bombed Egyptian airfields in the Canal Zone on 31 October. But the three allies proved to be in very vulnerable position. The USA and the United Nations were outraged by the aggression. With the climate of world opinion against them, the initiative, which was known as Operation Musketeer, withered. Far from being ousted from power, Nasser's position was cemented as an Arab hero. He stayed in power until his death on 28 September 1970.

Lt Col Pat de Clermont and Lt Col Philip Harrison were both elected at the business meeting held in December 1957. At a stroke, the club acquired the commitment and pleasure of two engaging characters. Lt Col de Clermont had won a DSO in Korea in 1952, where he served as a squadron leader with 8th King's Royal Hussars. Curiously, the award was gazetted on Tuesday 29 April 1952 when the only other recipient of the DSO announced that day was a friend of his, Major Roderick (Roddie) Robertson-Macleod, MC, of the King's Own Scottish Borderers.

Lt Col Pat de Clermont, member 1957–82

A mark of Lt Col de Clermont's style was evident in his wager with Mr Alastair Paton at his first dinner that Mr Paton would drink at Morris Hall one imperial pint of Krug 1949 within one hour of arrival. Mr Paton accepted the bet and was happy to lose.

Lt Col Harrison was less boisterous, but a most reliable friend to the members of the club in general, and to former and future servicemen in particular. He was the regimental secretary of the King's Own Scottish Borderers, based in the barracks in Berwick, where he maintained a generous and warm reception in his small officers' mess. He too had won a DSO in Korea in November 1951 when commanding B Company KOSB during the famous 'Guy Fawkes Battle' of 4/5 November at Kowang San. Sergeant Bill Speakman won a VC that night, and a subaltern, Willie (later Sir William) Purves, who went on to become the chairman of HSBC, won a DSO. The distinctive fact here is that it was the only DSO awarded to a national serviceman.

Sport was the focus of the majority of bets laid in the late 1950s, and leading up to and beyond the 1960 Rome Olympic Games. Major Home Robertson, whose daughter Georgina enjoyed being a support worker at those Games, bet Major Van Burdon that no one would jump higher than 7 feet. Major Home Robertson lost because a Russian, Robert Shavlakelze, jumped 7 ft 1 in, beating the Olympic record.

Major Home Robertson also bet Lt Col de Clermont that Dr Barbara Moore would not walk across America as forecast by her, and again he lost. Barbara Moore (1903–1977) was a Russian-born health enthusiast who gained fame or notoriety in the 1960s. She walked from John o'Groats to Land's End in twenty-three days in 1960, then undertook a forty-six-day, 3,387-mile walk from San Francisco to New York City, where she arrived on 6 July 1960.

Lt Col Lionel Machin bet Major Van Burdon in 1960 that the repairs to Coldstream Bridge would not be completed by 1 February 1961. Major Burdon lost, but this small bet conceals a greater interest. In 1959 exceptional rain created the biggest Tweed flood since 1948. The river rose so high that it covered the arches of Coldstream Bridge and there was genuine concern that the bridge would fail. In the event, it survived, but there was severe structural damage, which was repaired during 1960. The bridge was also widened marginally at the same time to create a footpath on both sides of the road.

Mr D. M. Marshall bet Lt Col Machin that in the Test matches against South Africa no bowler would take two wickets in consecutive balls in one over. Lt Col Machin did lose, although Geoff Griffin took the wicket of M. J. K. Smith with the last ball of one over and that of Peter Walker on the first ball of the next.

Dining at Tillmouth Park Hotel on 15 February 1961, Lt Col Horace Davidson bet Major Home Robertson that a man would be projected into space and come back alive and survive before 13 January 1962. Lt Col Davidson won rather quickly.

Less than two months elapsed before Lieutenant Yuri Gagarin, a

Russian pilot and cosmonaut, completed a single orbit of Earth on 12 April 1961. He was in space for 1 hour and 48 minutes, arguably the shortest time any celebrity has spent on achieving world-wide fame. He was only twenty-seven years old (born 9 March 1934). The publicity was not kind to him and his marriage suffered because of the huge number of female fans who sought his company, although his wife did stick with him. Alcohol also played a damaging role (he never drank before his space flight, but felt obliged to respond to toasts during his extensive ambassadorial trips to promote the Soviet Union). He died in an air crash on 27 March 1968.

The space race was on. At the next club dinner in 1962, Mr Alastair Paton bet Mr D. M. Marshall that (John) Glenn would not go into orbit. Glenn, born 18 July 1921, was a US Marine Corps pilot and astronaut. He later became a Democratic Senator for Ohio, and had the distinction of being the only astronaut to fly on both the Mercury and Space Shuttle programmes. He was also the oldest person to go into space when he flew on *Discovery* (STS-95) on 29 October 1998 at the age of 77. His first flight, though, was on *Friendship 7* which circled the Earth three times on 20 February 1962. The flight lasted 4 hours 55 minutes and 23 seconds. The citizens of Perth, Western Australia, lit every light possible to attract his attention on the first flight, and repeated the effort on his final flight in 1998.

Mr Allan Herriot was a little more adventurous when he bet Major Home Robertson that the planet Venus would be circumnavigated before the next dinner. In fact the feat was not achieved for more than twenty years.

The Soviet spacecraft *Venera 15* was launched on June 2, 1983 and reached orbit around Venus on October 10, 1983. The spacecraft was inserted into Venus orbit a day apart from *Venera 16,* with its orbital plane shifted by an angle of approximately 4° relative to the other probe. Together with *Venera 16*, the spacecraft charted the area from the North Pole down to about 30° N latitude (or approximately 25 per cent of Venus's surface) over the eight months of mapping operations.

The US *Magellan* spacecraft, named after the sixteenth-century Portuguese explorer whose expedition first circumnavigated the Earth, was launched on 4 May 1989, and arrived at Venus on 10 August 1990. It charted more than 98 per cent of Venus at a resolution of about 100 metres.

In a puckish mood, Lt Col Pat de Clermont bet Major Jock Home Robertson that Lt Col Philip Harrison would be discovered doing the twist at Paxton House on 3 August 1962. The twist became a craze when Chubby Checker made the eponymous song a hit in the Billboard Hot

100 in September 1960. It was a very lively dance, which briefly became popular again in the late 1980s. But the notion of Lt Col Harrison, a slow-moving, quite round bachelor officer, doing the twist remains hilariously unlikely fifty years later.

More soberly, Mr Lambert Carmichael bet Mr John Ridley that he would not give evidence at the Inquiry which was to be held by Lord Hunter. The Commission of Inquiry chaired by Lord Hunter was to report on drift netting for Scottish salmon and trout fisheries. It started in March 1962 and led to the abolition of all drift netting for salmon in Scottish waters. Mr Carmichael lost because Mr Ridley did give evidence.

The 1963 dinner was held at the Tillmouth Park Hotel, but only thirteen members managed to attend because deep snow covered the countryside and many roads were blocked.

Mr Lambert Carmichael showed a continuing interest in the space race when he bet Lt Col Harrison that someone would land on the Moon before the next dinner. Absurd as that seemed at the time, the scientists were working faster than most people realised and those living at the time will never forget the sense of great human achievement when Neil Armstrong stepped onto the surface of the Moon on 20 July 1969.

Mr John Ridley also bet Mr Allan Herriot that the USA would not put three men in orbit in one spacecraft. Although Mr Herriot lost, it became entirely normal for three or more people to be in one spacecraft (*Apollo 11*, the first Moon landing, had Armstrong, Aldrin and Collins on board).

Closer to home, Major Home Robertson bet Mr Bill McCreath that Harold Macmillan would not be prime minister on 15 January 1964. Macmillan had been prime minister since 1957. In what proved to be his final year in office, his government was rocked by the Vassall and Profumo scandals. Macmillan resigned prematurely on 18 October 1963 after a medical misdiagnosis, and lived out a long retirement as an elder statesman until his death on 29 December 1986.

Major Van Burdon must have been most satisfied to win his wager with Lt Col Horace Davidson that his bull, Freddie, would put forty heifers in calf. He scored forty-one.

After some years of rather pedestrian wagers, the club came alive in 1964. Politics played a large part, with bets about Alec Douglas-Home remaining as prime minister, Labour acquiring power, the likelihood of a General Election, the number of Liberal MPs in the Commons, whether Anthony (later Lord) Lambton would still be an MP, whether President de Gaulle would still be in post, that Southern Rhodesia would be independent, whether there would be a peace-keeping force in Cyprus and the chances of Archbishop Makarios still being in power.

At the annual business meeting in the officers' mess at the barracks in Berwick on 29 January 1965, Mr Alastair Paton and Lt Col Lionel Machin tendered their resignations. Mr Paton, a moderately successful horse trainer who was 6 ft 9 in tall, had been a member since 1936 and was well liked by his colleagues. He had outlasted all three of those who were elected to the club at the same time (Sir Charles Furness, Major Ronnie Bell and Mr Henry McCreath) by at least ten years.

Back in 1955 Mr Paton had started a chain of sixty-one wagers on activity at the Cheltenham Festival when he bet David Herriot that a horse called Tudor Bramble would win the Gold Cup. It would have been worrying for anyone with a horse in training with Mr Paton that he not only lost this bet, but also five of the six similar ones laid in subsequent years. In fact most of the fourteen members who have placed a bet on a result at Cheltenham have lost, other than Mr Ronald Barber, who has laid twenty-five bets, most of them with Richard Landale. He has won fourteen of them and lost six, while five recorded no result.

Lt Col Machin was elected to the Club in 1951. Born on 17 August 1893, he was commissioned into the King's Own Scottish Borderers on 17 February 1915. He served in Belgium, France and Italy, was mentioned in despatches in 1917 and won the Military Cross. After commanding the Regimental Depot at the end of the 1930s, he was appointed to command the 7th (Galloway) Battalion the King's Own Scottish Borderers in 1940, handing over command part way through 1942. He married Constance Gough in 1923 and, although we do not know when she died, he married secondly in 1968 Lois Barstow, who survived him by many years. He died on 3 April 1974.

These resignations opened two vacancies, one of which was offered to Dr Alan Bousfield, the nephew of the late former member, Dr Vincent Badcock. Dr Bousfield accepted and remained a member until 1981. The second vacancy was offered to Mr Archie MacArthur, who has the distinction of being the only person to join, resign and rejoin. He had been elected at the business meeting in 1953 and attended his first and only dinner in 1954. He apologised for missing every subsequent meeting until he formally resigned by the medium of a letter tabled at the business meeting on 15 December 1956. Late in 1964 he indicated to the secretary that he would very much like to rejoin the club if invited. He remained a member until 1982.

There was a full turnout for dinner in 1965, and seventy-nine bets were laid by the seventeen members. Sadly there is no record of who won or lost, although some of the sporting and political subjects would be verifiable today. But it would have been amusing to learn the outcome of some of the more personal wagers. For example, Lt Col Mark Leather bet Lt Col Horace Davidson that Kirsty (Davidson's wife) would say he had been drinking when he returned from the Salmon Club dinner. This bet had been laid before, and Mr Andrew Wailes-Fairbairn also repeated it on this evening. It is a racing certainty that Kirsty, who was a vigorous, amusing and much-loved member of the community (and a magistrate on the Bench with Lt Col Johnny Collingwood and Mr Allan Herriot) would have given Horace a real wigging for enjoying his dinner to the full.

Lt Col Leather went on to bet Lt Col Davidson that he would be seasick during 1965. Dr Bousfield challenged Lt Col de Clermont with two medical bets, the first that Lt Col de Clermont would not need an antibiotic during the year, and the second that he would not suffer from gout. We do not know if Dr Bousfield was his doctor, but the bets could be viewed as exhortations to behave, rather than a conviction about the result.

Major Jock Home Robertson achieved the most cryptic of wagers when he bet Lt Col Horace Davidson that at 8.00 am on 31 May 1965 the sun would be shining in deference to an important anniversary. According to his son, John Home Robertson, who served for thirty years as an MP and MSP, it was probably an allusion to the evacuation of Dunkirk between 26 May and 4 June 1940.

Lt Col Davidson's riposte was to challenge Major Home Robertson that he would not have an article of fiction published in *CGA Magazine* by 31 January 1966, and in a supplementary challenge, that he would not have an article or letter printed under his own name in *The Times*.

At the 1966 dinner, Mr Andrew Wailes-Fairbairn bet Lt Col Johnny Collingwood that he would not play his hurdy-gurdy at a public occasion during 1966. Back in 1954 Lt Col Collingwood had found amongst the mountains of furniture stored in his stables a magnificent old barrel organ, which he placed under the veranda on the east side of Cornhill House. All visitors were encouraged to play it, and it was normally put to good use at the annual church fete. But evidently Lt Col Collingwood claimed that he did not play it himself, and he lost the bet.

On the political front, Britain was struggling to manage the ambitions of Southern Rhodesia under its leader, Ian Smith. Mr Andrew Wailes-Fairbairn bet Mr Bill McCreath that Rhodesia would be a republic by January 1967 and Mr John Ridley bet Lt Col Philip Harrison that Smith would still be in power by 30 May 1966. Mr Wailes-Fairbairn and Lt Col Harrison lost their bets.

Southern Rhodesia was a self-governing colony of the United Kingdom until it made a unilateral declaration of independence (UDI) on 11 November 1965. Smith did remain the leader of the government, but the international community was most reluctant to recognise the 'new' state, and the United Nations Security Council imposed sanctions, which were not universally recognised. On 2 March 1970 the Rhodesian government formally severed links with the British Crown, to which it had remained loyal up to that time, and declared a republic.

Mr Archie McArthur challenged Lt Col Pat de Clermont that there would be a recognised cease-fire in Vietnam under supervision of the UNO (United Nations Organization) or similar force before 1 February 1967. Mr McArthur lost.

The Vietnam War, which took place in (the then) North and South Vietnam, Laos and Cambodia, lasted for twenty years from November 1955 until the fall of Saigon to the North Vietnamese on 30 April 1975. The conflict owed its roots to the French Empire, which began its conquest of South-East Asia in the late 1850s. During the Second World War there was an uneasy collaboration between the (Vichy) French and invading Japanese, which fell apart with the unconditional surrender of Japan in August 1945. Ho Chi Minh, the leader of the Viet Minh (North Vietnamese), declared the Independent Republic of Vietnam on 2 September 1945. The USA, Soviet Union and United Kingdom agreed that the region belonged to France and determined to help them to secure their dominion.

From 1950 to 1954 the French relied extensively upon American support. Indeed, some reports claim that 80 per cent of the cost of the war with the Viet Minh was paid by the USA. The Soviet Union backed the North. Eventually the French suffered a catastrophic defeat at the battle of Dien Bien Phu in May 1954. At the subsequent Geneva Conference, the French negotiated a cease-fire agreement with the Viet Minh. Independence was granted to Cambodia, Laos and Vietnam.

The USA couldn't help itself. Fearing the rolling tide of communism, it steadily increased its commitment to support South Vietnam, particularly under the government of President Lyndon Johnson. Ultimately 58,169 Americans died in the conflict, which became deeply unpopular at home. The estimated overall casualties were 5,773,190, of whom an estimated 2,122,244 died. (There is a fuller evaluation on http://www.103fieldbatteryraa.net/documents/74.html)

Mr John Ridley bet Lt Col Johnny Collingwood, who was then chairman of the Berwick Bench, that a breathalyser test would be law by 31 January 1967. Mr Ridley lost. Mr Bill McCreath bet Mr Michael Lyndon Skeggs that no one in England would be convicted as a result of a breathalyser test by 31 December 1966, and Mr Skeggs lost. And Mr McCreath bet Dr Alan Bousfield that he would not attend at any police station to adjudicate on a drunk in charge or driving case in 1966. This was lost by Mr McCreath because doctors still had to evaluate drink driving, even though the breathalyser was not formally in use.

The Road Safety Act of 1967 introduced the first legal maximum blood alcohol (drink driving) limit in the United Kingdom. The limit was set at a maximum BAC (blood alcohol concentration) of 80 mg of alcohol per 100 ml of blood, or the equivalent 107 milligrams of alcohol per 100 millilitres of urine. It became an offence to drive, attempt to drive or be in charge of a motor vehicle with a blood alcohol concentration that exceeded the maximum prescribed legal limit. The breathalyser was first used in earnest on 8 October 1967.

At the business meeting on 23 January 1967, the members decided that Mr Ilay Campbell, later Sir Ilay Campbell, Bt, should be asked to fill the vacancy left by the sudden death of Lt Col Mark Leather. They decided to hold the dinner at the Collingwood Arms again, and devised a menu which included green turtle soup, salmon, roast turkey with chestnut and sausage stuffing supplemented by chipolata sausages, soft roes in bacon and an unspecified dessert to round it off. They intended to drink Cockburn '47 port and cognac to enjoy with their cigars.

Members laid 115 wagers that night, most of them sporting and political. Mr Michael Skeggs extended the thinking by betting Mr Andrew Wailes-Fairbairn that (Francis) Chichester would have a disaster with his cask of beer before he reached Plymouth. It seems that Mr Skeggs lost that, although it is hard to discover anything about the cask of beer so many years after the event. Then Mr Wailes-Fairbairn bet Mr Ross Logan that Chichester would reach England in his yacht under his own steam. Happily Mr Logan lost. Finally Lt Col Horace Davidson lost his bet with Mr Bill McCreath that Chichester would not reach England without putting in at a port on his journey back from Australia.

Francis Chichester departed Plymouth in his yacht, *Gypsy Moth IV*, on 27 August 1966. It took him 226 days of sailing, with one stop in Sydney, to become the first person ever to circumnavigate the globe solo from west to east via the great capes. He arrived back in Plymouth on 28 May 1967 and a few weeks later the Queen, in a spectacularly thoughtful and imaginative initiative, knighted him using the same sword that Queen Elizabeth I had used to knight Sir Francis Drake. Drake and his crew were the first Englishmen to circumnavigate the globe between 1577 and 1580.

Lt Col Philip Harrison bet Lt Col Johnny Collingwood that Jim

Clark would be the 1967 champion Grand Prix driver. Lt Col Harrison lost.

Jim Clark, who was born in Fife, was regarded very much as a local boy because he lived outside Duns and was educated in Chirnside. He was a highly versatile racing driver, who competed in sports and touring cars and raced in the Indianapolis 500, which he won in 1965. He was killed in a Formula Two motor racing accident in Hockenheim, Germany in 1968. At the time of his death, he had won more Grand Prix races (twenty-five) and achieved more Grand Prix pole positions (thirty-three) than any other driver. He was world champion in 1963 and 1965.

Lt Col Collingwood was on a mission in 1968. He was deeply concerned about the impact of the breathalyser on the ability of the club to continue in its traditional form. He sought to persuade members that they should vote for his recommended reform at the AGM (alas, the nature of that reform is not clear from the records), and he feared that members would not be ready to enjoy an extended evening because their wives would always wish to collect them early. Interestingly, the mood was against him and he lost all of the wagers relating to reform.

Major Jock Home Robertson bet Mr John Ridley that Great Britain's reputation as a staunch upholder of the Olympic spirit would be triumphantly vindicated in her failure to bring home a gold medal from Mexico. Major Home Robertson lost.

Great Britain won gold medals in the 400 metres hurdles (David Hemery with a world record of 48.1 seconds), middleweight boxing (Chris Finnegan), shooting (Bob Braithwaite), sailing (Rodney Pattison and Ian MacDonald Smith), and the equestrian team took the team gold medal in the three-day event.

Dr Alan Bousfield bet Mr Allan Herriot that no ship would run aground in the Tweed before 31 January 1969. Dr Bousfield's loss was emphatic because there were two in one day!

It must have been disappointing and irritating for those members who attended dinner at the Castle Hotel on 17 February 1969. Almost half of the team, eight members, failed to turn up. One of the missing people was Mr Ross Logan, who wrote to say that he wished to resign. He had failed to appear on three previous occasions, so only attended seven dinners during his ten years of membership. He had laid or received thirty-three wagers during his time in the club, winning fourteen and losing nineteen.

During the evening, Mr Allan Herriot bet Mr Lambert Carmichael that 'test tubes would be out genetically'. Mr Bill McCreath also bet Lt Col Horace Davidson that no further announcement of any advancement in test tube babies would be announced by anybody of repute.

There was great public interest in the research into in vitro fertilisation. Dr Patrick Steptoe, a gynaecologist at Oldham General Hospital, and Dr Robert Edwards, a physiologist at Cambridge University, had been actively working on finding an alternative solution for conception since 1966. Though Drs Steptoe and Edwards had successfully found a way to fertilise an egg outside a woman's body, they were still troubled by problems after replacing the fertilised egg back into the woman's uterus.

By 1977, all of the pregnancies resulting from their procedure (about eighty) had lasted only a few short weeks. But on July 25, 1978 Louise Joy Brown, the world's first successful 'test-tube baby' was born in Great Britain. Though the technology that made her conception possible was heralded as a triumph in medicine and science, it also caused many to consider the possibilities of future ill-use.

Mr Allan Herriot laid another wager with Lt Col Philip Harrison. He bet that *Concorde* (Anglais) would fly by 30 September 1969. The records show that he lost, but he should have won because Brian Trubshaw flew the British-built *Concorde* from RAF Fairford on 9 April 1969. The French version, *Concorde 01*, was flown by test pilot Andre Turcat on 2 March 1969.

Lord Michael Joicey bet Lt Col Johnny Collingwood that Mike Ansell would not catch more than one fish during his February stay with Lt Col Collingwood. Lord Joicey lost because he caught three. 'So what', the reader might ask.

Colonel Sir Michael Ansell, who was born on 26 March 1905, was a truly remarkable man. Like his father before him, and his son after him, he was commissioned into the 5th Royal Inniskilling Dragoon Guards. His father, Lt Col George Ansell, was killed while commanding the regiment at the Battle of Nery on 1 September 1914, and is buried in a French cemetery some five miles from the battlefield. L Battery RHA won three Victoria Crosses in the engagement.

Mike Ansell, who was awarded a DSO in 1944, the CBE in 1951, then knighted in 1968, was completely blinded by friendly fire during the retreat from the Somme to St Valery in June 1940 while he was commanding the Lothian and Border Yeomanry. The regiment was part of 51st Division trying to embark on ships to be evacuated then reinserted at Le Havre to continue the fight. With no vessels available, the divisional commander ordered his troops to surrender. Determined to escape, Ansell with a few companions took shelter for the night in the loft of a barn. A party of English soldiers later entered the barn and, believing the occupants above them to be Germans, discharged a hail of fire upwards. Lt Col Ansell, blinded and severely wounded in the hand, was subsequently taken prisoner and underwent agonising and prolonged treatment in unavailing efforts to save his eyes. He spent the next three years in a prisoner-of-war camp. It was during those years that he began to put together his ideas about promoting equestrianism as a spectator sport after the war.

Repatriated in 1943, he took up horticulture, and typically, was soon winning prizes. Still in his early forties, and with personal international experience, he was invited to become chairman of the British Showjumping Association. He proceeded to transform the sport's public image.

As far as possible he acted as if he were not blind at all, and talked quite naturally about 'seeing' people, or 'watching' competitions. He developed a formidable memory and an uncanny way of sensing what was going on around him. He grasped every opportunity to promote equestrian sport, and shrewdly realised that show jumping was suitable for television.

An old friend of Johnny Collingwood, he visited Cornhill every year to fish on the Tweed. The author of this brief history used to watch in awe as the ghillie started each visit by putting a tin can on the lawn at Cornhill House before directing Mike Ansell to cast at it. With a little bit of shuffling around, 'the Colonel' was soon consistently hitting the can. He and the ghillie would then go down to the river, climb into the boat and start fishing. Thanks to the practice on the lawn, the boat could be accurately placed to ensure that the cast went where it was supposed to: an example of fantastic teamwork.

Bets about man landing on the Moon started in 1966. By February 1969, there was a keener sense of anticipation. Lt Col Horace Davidson bet Mr Allan Herriot that no human would land on the Moon. At the same time, Lt Col Philip Harrison bet Lord Joicey that the Russians would also put a man on the Moon (clearly anticipating that the Americans would do so anyway). Mr Bill McCreath bet Lt Col Collingwood that anyone who did land would not live for more than twenty-four hours. The excitement was justified because the *Apollo 11* mission, which was launched from Earth on 16 July 1969, placed Neil Armstrong, followed by Buzz Aldrin, on the Moon on 20 July 1969. Armstrong's immortal words on stepping onto the lunar surface were 'That's one small step for man, one giant leap for mankind.'

Seventeen members attended the dinner at the Tillmouth Park Hotel on 16

February 1970. Mr Billy Straker-Smith, who had been elected to replace Mr Ross Logan, apologised for failing to attend because he was ill. In the event, he attended the dinner on only two occasions, in 1971 and 1973, although he evidently remained a member because he apologised formally for failing to attend in 1978. The records show no resignation, and there is no further mention of him after 1978.

Mr Straker-Smith merits historical mention as one of the co-founders of the Tweed Foundation, arguably the most important contribution to river management in the world. He would be less enthusiastic to be remembered also as a gambling man who once lost a fortune during an evening of cards in London. But there is a good story, probably apocryphal, about Billy and his father Tom, who conceived a plan to tidy up the churchyard at Carham, where the gravestones lay flat or at angles in a thoroughly untidy and sloppy way. They solemnly moved what they could so that a large number of memorials were leaning against the two walls that led the length of the cemetery. It only occurred to them at this late stage that this left no way to be confident about the position of the graves. Tom was concerned about his long-term resting place, so he arranged for his grave to be dug in a plum site overlooking a stretch of the adjacent River Tweed. He was furious when he discovered that his son Billy was using it as a butt from which to shoot duck, leaving the empty cartridge cases to fill the convenient hole.

Seals exercised the minds of members in 1971. Mr Tony Barber lost his bet with Mr Bill McCreath that Mr McCreath would not see a salmon caught by a seal from his office window before the end of 1971. Dr Alan Bousfield successfully bet Lt Col Horace Davidson that before the next dinner Dr Bousfield would not see a seal in Berwick with a salmon in its mouth. Dr Bousfield then bet Mr Michael Skeggs that there would be a cull of seals on the Farne Islands before the next dinner, while Major Van Burdon bet Mr Allan Herriot that there would not be such a cull. Dr Bousfield and Mr Herriot lost, although in August 1971 the National Trust announced that 3,000 grey seal calves and their mothers were to be killed on the Farne Islands over three years. It was the biggest ever cull undertaken by the National Trust to address the problems of over-crowding.

Seal culls were banned in 1978 after a public outcry when seal pups were shown being slaughtered on television.

Major Van Burdon bet Mr Bill McCreath that Britain would be in the Common Market by 31 January 1972. He lost, but he also bet Lt Col Horace Davidson that Common Market countries (in the event of Great

Britain joining) would be allowed to drift-net for salmon off the Berwick-shire–Northumberland coast. Again, he lost. Mr Andrew Wailes-Fairbairn lost his bet with Sir Ilay Campbell that by 1 February 1972, the United Kingdom would not be committed to joining the Common Market.

Geoffrey Rippon was the chief negotiator for the terms of Britain's entry into the Common Market. Agreement in principle was achieved in 1971, although Great Britain, Ireland and Denmark did not become fully fledged members until 31 December 1972.

On 15 February 1972 Dr Alan Bousfield bet Mr Michael Skeggs that Mr Skeggs' wife would be chairman of Northumberland County Council before the next dinner. Although Dr Bousfield lost, Barbara Lyndon Skeggs did pursue an energetic and effective role in local government, for which she was awarded an MBE. She sat on the Berwick Bench as a magistrate, becoming deputy chairman and resigned after being nominated as the first female high sheriff for the County of Northumberland, a role which she filled for a year from April 1994. Subsequently she became a deputy lieutenant of the county before retiring with her husband to the north of Scotland to be closer to her daughter.

The club can boast five high sheriffs: Mr David Askew in 1912, Mr Billy Straker Smith in 1967, Mr Tom Sale in 1985, Sir Michael Blake in 2002 and Mr Eric Grounds in 2006. They have also had one lord lieu-tenant, Mr Alexander Trotter, who has been the father of the club since 2005, having attended his first dinner in 1973.

That same evening, Sir Ilay Campbell bet Lt Col Philip Harrison that the situation in Northern Ireland would be resolved by January 1973. Sir Ilay was spectacularly wrong.

In August 1969 there were extensive riots across Northern Ireland. Between 14 and 17 August eight people died and 133 were treated for shotgun wounds. The British Army was formally deployed for the first time since the end of the Second World War. On 11 October three people were shot dead in the Protestant Shankhill area of Belfast, two by the army, and one RUC officer shot by loyalists. The trouble continued through 1970, with rubber bullets being fired for the first time on 2 August 1970. On 6 February 1971, Private Robert Curtis became the first soldier to die when he was shot by Republican terrorists in the New Lodge Road, Belfast.

Operation Demetrius was launched on 9 August 1971. The security forces arrested 342 people suspected of being involved in paramilitary activity in order to intern them. Over the next three days the army shot fourteen civilians and three soldiers were shot dead by republicans.

Matters escalated over the ensuing months, and on 30 January 1972, Bloody Sunday saw twenty-seven civilians shot by the army during a civil rights march in Londonderry.

There followed thirty-five years of intermittent violence. In the period 1969 to 1999, 3,296 individuals died because of 'the Troubles'. Of these, 957 were military and 2,339 civilian. It was not until 31 July 2007 that Operation Banner, the formal title of the British Army campaign in Ulster, officially ended.

Lt Col Johnny Collingwood bet Mr Allan Herriot that Alec Douglas-Home's formula for Rhodesia's immediate future would be accepted/implemented. Unfortunately Lt Col Collingwood lost.

Negotiations with Ian Smith's Rhodesian government rumbled on through 1971, with a written agreement being signed on 24 November. In order to secure international recognition, Smith accepted the principle of majority rule in the long term. But full agreement was contingent upon the approval of the population, and it swiftly became apparent that the majority of Africans rejected the proposals.

Lt Col Collingwood then bet Mr Herriot that the existing strike of the National Union of Miners (NUM) would end peacefully by the end of February 1972. Mr Herriot lost. Several other members laid wagers along the same lines.

The 1972 miners' strike was their first national strike since 1926. On 5 January the union's national executive rejected the offer of a small rise. Two days later, the National Coal Board withdrew all offers made over the previous three months. Miners downed tools on 9 January. The action spread from coal power stations to cover all power stations, steelworks, ports and coal depots. Dockers in Newport and Cardiff refused to unload coal. On 21 January the NUM decided to try to stop the movement of all fuel supplies. The Government declared a state of emergency on 9 February, which led to the declaration of a three-day week from 11 February in an effort to conserve electricity. There were frequent power cuts. Hard bargaining followed and agreement was reached on 19 February. Picketing was called off and the miners accepted a deal by ballot on 25 February, returning to work on 28 February.

Lt Col Philip Harrison successfully bet Sir Ilay Campbell that by January 1973, Malta would have acceded to the NATO bid.

For several years after independence in 1964, Malta followed a policy of close cooperation with the United Kingdom and other NATO countries. This changed with the election of the Malta Labour Party in June 1971. The NATO headquarters in Malta was closed, and the US Sixth Fleet discontinued recreational visits to the country. Several NATO countries (including the USA) substantially increased their financial contribution to Malta, which allowed British forces to remain in Malta until 1979.

1973 marks the start of a new period because the current father of the club, Mr Alexander Trotter, attended his first dinner that year. All of the current members were alive and most would remember the events registered through the wagers. This should add colour and texture to the written record.

The first three wagers laid, rather than accepted by Mr Trotter, were:

- With Mr Andrew Wailes-Fairbairn that the North Northumberland Hunt would kill more foxes between 1 November 1973 and 1 January 1974 than between the same period in 1972/73. Mr Trotter won: in 1972/73 it killed three brace, and in 1973/74, three and a half brace.
- With Lt Col Pat de Clermont that water rationing in Berwickshire would cease by 1 June 1973. Mr Trotter lost this one: it finished on 1 December 1973.
- With Mr Allan Herriot that the sterling value of the dollar on 15 January 1974, as in the *Financial Times*, would not be less than $2.40. Mr Trotter lost this one too: it was $2.19.

From a purely statistical perspective, a quick check of the records shows that Mr Trotter has laid 135 wagers and accepted 107 during his forty years in the club.

Lt Col Horace Davidson's bet with Mr Tom Sale on 15 February 1974 that Mr Sale would not sell an estate or farm for more than £1,000 per acre provides the opportunity to look at land prices over the years (see overleaf).

That same evening, Mr Douglas Skeggs bet Mr Lambert Carmichael that five-star petrol would exceed 55 p per gallon in 1974/75. Mr Carmichael lost. This begs for a summary of petrol prices. According to a House of Commons Research Paper 'A century of change: trends in UK statistics from 1900':

- In 1902 a gallon of (the equivalent of) four-star petrol cost £2.50.
- In 1909 a consumer tax of 3 pence (at 1909 values, which equates

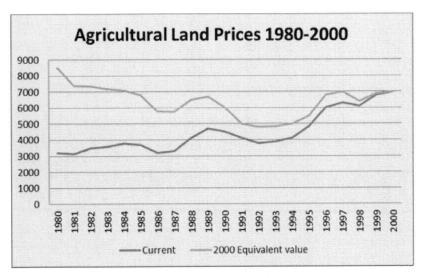

Data drawn from the University of Exeter Centre for Rural Research paper by DM Winter:Rural Policy: New Directions and New Challenges, February 2002. Prices in £s per hectare.

to 61 p at 1999 values) was applied. That was doubled in 1915, but totally removed in 1921.

- In 1916, the modern-day price equivalent was a whopping £6.65 per gallon.
- Petrol was cheapest in 1928 and 1949, when the 1999 comparative cost was £1.77 per gallon and £1.92 respectively.
- After the Suez War in 1957 the cost was £4.16.
- In 2011 the average price of a gallon of petrol is £6.21.

All prices are adjusted to represent 1999 values, except where noted.

Mr Bill McCreath bet Mr Michael Skeggs that Jeremy Thorpe, leader of the Liberal Party, would not retain his seat in the General Election. Mr McCreath lost. Thorpe and the Liberals enjoyed a much better result than they did in the 1970 election, when they lost seven seats (thereby retaining only six). Thorpe himself squeezed in by a narrow majority. Between 1972 and 1974 the Liberals scored a series of by-election victories, and in the 1974 General Election they secured 19.3 per cent of the popular vote, returning to a hung parliament with fourteen seats. This forced the Conservative prime minister, Edward Heath, to consider a coalition with the Liberals. He tried to make a deal with Thorpe, offering him the position of home secretary. Thorpe feared that his party would not fully support him, and he sought to wring guarantees from Heath about electoral reform. The deal fell apart, paving the way for Harold Wilson to form a Labour government.

To the dismay of all, Lt Col Johnny Collingwood died at the relatively youthful age of sixty-nine in April 1975. Members decided to elect Mr Neil Maconochie of Horncliffe House in his place. Mr Maconochie was a member for only a short time, attending his first dinner in February 1976 and his last in 1980. He was not present at the 1981 dinner and his name was not mentioned in the records until his formal resignation was noted at the business meeting in 1982. According to two members who were present in 1980, Mr Maconochie arrived at dinner heavily 'primed'. It did not take long for him to slide slowly below the table, totally unconscious. Lt Col de Clermont, who was capable of consuming prodigious amounts of alcohol, but who never showed the effects, was infuriated, not least because he regarded Mr Maconochie's behaviour as a breach of trust and friendship. It seems that during the Second World War, Lt Col de Clermont sent cases of champagne to Mr Maconochie and his regiment in Burma. Two members were detailed to take him home immediately and when he awoke, he learned that he would be expected to resign.

Mr Maconochie was liberal with his wagers – both taken and laid. There is one that is more intriguing than most. In 1977, Mr Andrew Wailes-Fairbairn bet that Mr Maconochie would have had a major difference of opinion with Tiny Rowland by 31 January 1978. Mr Maconochie lost. Although nobody can recall what relationship the two may have had, it seems that Maconochie may have worked for Lonrho where Rowland was chief executive. At a later date the Maconochie family suffered a ghastly tragedy when Mrs Maconochie fell through a skylight in their London house and died as a result.

Dinner was abandoned on 15 February 1978 because too many members were snowed in. Instead, they met at the Turret Hotel on 1 March. Sadly none of the bets were recorded that night. The club experienced other difficulties during this period, with the business meeting on 5 December 1978 being adjourned to 18 December because of the low attendance. Even then, five members were not present. And the dinner on 15 February 1979 suffered because of bad weather again, preventing seven members from attending. The eleven members who did attend laid fifty-six wagers, but none of the results were recorded. Nevertheless, we can still track down the missing information.

The most interesting bet involved Jeremy Thorpe again. Lt Col de Clermont bet Mr Michael Skeggs that Jeremy Thorpe would be convicted, and he lost.

Thorpe was leader of the Liberal Party until his resignation in 1976. He was tainted by an accusation by one Norman Scott that they had engaged in a homosexual affair, which Thorpe robustly rejected. Thorpe and three other men were charged with conspiracy to murder after a bungled assassination attempt of Scott on a deserted moor in Southern England.

All the defendants were found not guilty. It took the jury fifteen hours of deliberation spread over three days to reach its verdict. Thorpe was also acquitted on a charge of inciting one of his co-defendants, David Holmes, to murder Scott. The trial lasted thirty-one days but Mr Thorpe's ordeal began when he was charged in August 1978.

Mr Richard Landale was feeling feisty that night. First he bet Mr Archie MacArthur that Mr MacArthur would be an illegitimate grandfather in 1979, and second he bet Lt Col Horace Davidson that he would have a black niece-in-law by 1980. He lost both wagers.

World affairs were in sharp focus with Mr Allan Herriot in February 1980. He bet Mr Landale that the USSR Red Army would reach the shore of the Indian Ocean. Linked with this, he bet Mr MacArthur that the Olympic Games would be cancelled.

The background was that Russia had invaded Afghanistan in 1979. Like every invader before them, they found that the Afghans were far tougher to beat than they imagined, and the Soviet Army experienced terrible casualties over the next ten years until they pulled out in 1989. But they did not try to advance to the Indian Ocean, so Mr Herriot was wrong.

Four wagers about the Soviet presence in Afghanistan were laid between 1980 and 1987, after which there was a prolonged silence until 2001, when Mr Terence Pardoe bet Mr Andrew Joicey that the USA would bomb a country other than Afghanistan before 31 December 2002.

The Olympic Games of 1980 were to be held in Moscow, and at one point it looked as if they might be abandoned as a number of countries, most notably the USA, boycotted the event in protest at the invasion of Afghanistan. Sadly the Russians decided to engage in tit-for-tat diplomacy by boycotting the subsequent Los Angeles Olympics in 1984.

Great Britain did take part, winning five gold medals, seven silver and nine bronze. Alan Wells won the 100 metres sprint and took silver in the 200 metres. Steve Ovett won gold in the 800 metres (and bronze in the 1,500 metres), Sebastian Coe gold in the 1500 metres (and silver in the 800 metres). Daley Thompson won the decathlon, and Duncan Goodhew took the gold in the 100 metres breaststroke.

Mr Allan Herriot bet Mr Michael Lyndon Skeggs that Robert Mugabe would have completely assumed power in Zimbabwe/Rhodesia.

At the end of the war in 1979, Mugabe emerged as a hero for many Africans. He won the general election of 1980 and became the first prime minister of Zimbabwe, after calling for reconciliation between formerly warring parties, including white Rhodesians and rival political groups. It is probably fair to comment that his first ten or eleven years in office marked a period of benign progress.

Modern readers will know that this idyll did not endure. Power proved to be a profound corrupter of Mugabe, whose policies and practices ruined his country and community. The land reform programme initiated in 2000, was particularly disastrous, and what was once a flourishing agricultural economy now lies in ruins.

Mr Lyndon Skeggs also bet Mr Neil Maconochie that the Dalai Lama would return to Tibet. In 1959, with the brutal suppression of the Tibetan national uprising in Lhasa by Chinese troops, the Dalai Lama was forced to escape into exile. Since then he has been living in Dharamsala, northern India, the seat of the Tibetan political administration in exile. During 1980 he made visits to northern towns of India and to Italy, Canada, the USA and Japan – but not to Tibet.

Finally, Mr Lyndon Skeggs bet Mr Andrew Wailes-Fairbairn that we would hear the last of the government by ayatollahs in Iran. He was far too optimistic. After the revolution which unseated the Shah in 1979, Ayatollah Khomeini returned to Tehran from exile on 1 February 1979. He was greeted by a rapturous crowd of several million. He did not wholly succeed in grasping the reins of power, and Iran was in political turmoil until 1983. Nevertheless, the ayatollahs wrested power from all opposition and remain the most powerful influence in the country even now (2011).

Lt Col Pat de Clermont bet Mr Allan Herriot that gold would reach $1,000 before 31 January 1981. In fact gold hit a new record of $850 per ounce in January 1980. It then plummeted and stayed in the $300–400 range for some years. In the late days of 2011, the price was in the range from $1,720 to $1,734 per ounce.

Lord Michael Joicey introduced an interesting mystery when he bet Mr Neil Maconochie that the origin of the tunnel at Horncliffe House would not be found. A tunnel at Horncliffe House? Sadly no one is able to shed light on the subject.

Mr Alexander Trotter bet Mr Alick Hay that on 1 February 1981 the assumed rate of inflation would not be more than 13½ per cent. On the day that the bet was laid, inflation was 14.18 per cent, and it averaged 13.58 per cent for the calendar year of 1980. But on 1 February 1981 it was down to 11.41 per cent, and the average for the calendar year was 10.35 per cent. Just for interest, the average figures for succeeding decades were: 1991, 4.25 per cent; 2001, 2.83 per cent, and for the first ten months of 2011, 3.15 per cent and rising.

Mr David Hotham laid three very different wagers on the night of 16 February 1981. He bet Mr Allan Herriot that *The Times* would survive recognisably; he bet Mr Michael Skeggs that Mr Skeggs would not see a badger by daylight, and he returned to Mr Herriot to bet that Prince Charles would marry Lady Diana Spencer. He proved to be right on all three counts.

Mr Hotham was a member of the club from 1980 to 1997. He had spent his working life as a correspondent for *The Times* and the *Economist*, notably in Turkey and Vietnam. He spent eight years in Ankara, spoke fluent Turkish, and published two books about the country and its people (*The Turks*, October 1972, and *Turkey*, August 1977). He inherited Milne Graden from his mother, who had married John Beaumont Hotham in 1905. John Hotham's father, an admiral of the Fleet, had acquired the property through marriage to Margaret Home, daughter of David Milne Home of Paxton and Milne Graden.

On 15 February 1982 Mr Andrew Wailes-Fairbairn bet Mr Alick Hay that Mr Hay would not recover any of his clocks that had been stolen that day, and sadly he was right. Mr Hay's mother was still resident in Duns Castle but away on holiday, while he and his wife were in accommodation in the stable yard. The castle had no alarms, and burglars broke in and stole three clocks, which were never recovered. Mr Hay claimed on insurance and with the proceeds replaced two clocks and added a painting.

Lord Joicey was a member of the club from 1960 to 1992. He had construction on his mind in 1982 when he bet Mr Michael Skeggs that he would not be able to cross the new Inverness–Black Isle bridge in 1982. Lord Joicey lost. He also bet Mr Skeggs that no four-wheel vehicle would cross the new Berwick bypass bridge. This time Mr Skeggs lost. But Sir David Burnett turned the tables by successfully betting Lord Joicey that Twizel Bridge would not be open for traffic before 1 January 1983.

Twizel Bridge is an interesting structure of great historical interest. It was probably built about 1500 AD and is widely accepted as one of the routes used by the English troops crossing the River Till on their way to the Battle of Flodden in 1513. It consists of a single 27 m (90 ft) arch springing from wide abutments, which was the greatest single span of any bridge in England when it was built. It is said that the supporting pillars rest on wool bales.

The medieval bridge was slightly altered in the eighteenth century when the grounds of Twizel Castle were landscaped. The bridge was closed to vehicular traffic in 1983 because it has a 30-degree angle at the eastern end, which created enormous difficulties for the large lorries of the twentieth century. A modern road bridge was built alongside.

After dinner on 15 February 1983, Mr Allan Herriot bet Mr Bill McCreath that 'Shergar would be able'. This brief allusion to a racehorse concealed a most interesting story. Mr Herriot lost and, although no one knew it at the time, the horse was already dead and buried.

Just one week earlier, at 8.30 pm on 8 February 1983, the doorbell rang in the house of Jim Fitzgerald, the head groom of the Ballymany Stud. Three armed and masked men barged in, saying that they had come for Shergar and they wanted a ransom of £2 million for him.

Shergar was five years old and preparing for his second season as a breeding stallion. As a two and three-year-old on the racecourse, the horse had been absolutely sensational. He won the 1981 Derby by ten lengths. Owned originally by the Aga Khan, he was syndicated for £10 million with forty shares, each of £250,000. The Aga Khan himself retained six shares. In his first season Shergar covered thirty-five mares at a cost of £80,000 each, and he was due to cover fifty-five mares in 1983.

The theft caused uproar. The IRA were strongly suspected as the culprits, and in a country that holds horses in the highest esteem, most people judged that they had made an enormous mistake. It did not take too long for the IRA to share that view, as the Gardaí and Northern Ireland police ransacked every conceivable hide in their hunt for the horse. It certainly hindered IRA activity, and they lost several arms caches in the process.

But no one ever saw Shergar again. Most commentators believed that he had been killed and buried, but no one could prove it. Andrew Alderson, the chief reporter of the *Telegraph*, wrote a lengthy exposé on 27 January 2008. He asserted that Kevin Mallon, a senior IRA leader and convicted killer, was the man who had devised the plot, which was fully sanctioned by the Provisional IRA Council. But four days after the theft, they instructed the gang to release the horse. By then Mallon realised that he was under surveillance, so he ordered that the horse should be shot. Two members of his team went with a machine gun and butchered the poor horse in its remote stable. The body is believed to be buried in a large bog.

Mr Richard Landale enjoyed a timely wager with the newly elected Mr Ian McCreath in 1984 that there would be 460 or more 'stiffs' reported to the coroner in 1984. Mr McCreath, who was then the North Northumberland coroner, lost the bet. It is not clear if Mr Landale was aware of the newly published Coroners' Rules 1984, which were due to become operational on 1 July. Mr Ronald Barber also successfully bet Mr McCreath that Mr McCreath would be mentioned in forty-five editions of the *Tweeddale Press* during 1984/85.

Mr Landale also acknowledged Mr McCreath's role as a governor of Longridge Towers School by betting him that the school would have 172 or more pupils by 1 August 1984. Mr McCreath will have been content to lose. The school used to be run by nuns, who slowly allowed the business side of school management to falter, with a consequent loss of pupils and status. A group of parents and local businessmen realised that the school should be a major asset for North Northumberland, so they undertook to save it. They did a wonderful job and the school continues to flourish in 2012, with boys and girls able to benefit from a full education.

It would have been astonishing if the miners' strike of 1984/85 had not been mentioned in the club's deliberations. Mr Michael Lyndon Skeggs bet Mr Bill Thomson (of Cessford) that the strike would finish by the end of February 1985. He was wrong, but Mr Alexander Trotter won his wager with Mr McCreath that the National Union of Mineworkers would instruct their members to work by 15 March 1985. In fact they received that instruction on 5 March. In a further dimension to these bets, Mr Thomson bet Sir Michael Blake that Margaret Thatcher would not be prime minister by February 1986.

The strike was a defining moment in British industrial relations, and its defeat significantly weakened the British trades union movement. It was recognised as a major political and ideological victory for Margaret Thatcher and the Conservative Party. Had the Government backed down, Mrs Thatcher would almost certainly have gone.

The strike became a symbolic struggle, since the NUM was one of the strongest unions in the country, generally thought to have brought down the Heath government by its 1974 strike. This time the Thatcher government stood firm and was able to consolidate its free-market programme. The political power of the NUM was broken permanently. The dispute exposed deep divisions in British society and caused considerable bitterness, especially in Northern England and in Wales.

Two wagers jump out of the records for 1987. First, Mr Eric Grounds bet Mr Andrew Douglas-Home that the customs authorities' estimate of the real casualty figure for the recent Townsend Thoresen disaster (nearer 200 than 100) would be proved accurate. Mr Grounds won.

Townsend Thoresen's car and passenger ferry, the MS *Herald of Free Enterprise*, was a roll-on roll-off vessel commissioned to work on the Dover to Calais cross-channel route. The ferry capsized on the night of 6 March 1987, moments after leaving the Belgian port of Zeebrugge, which was not part of her normal route. This proved to be a factor in the accident, which killed 193 passengers and crew.

The linkspan at Zeebrugge had not been designed specifically for vessels like the *Herald of Free Enterprise*: it used a single deck, preventing the simultaneous loading of two decks, and the ramp could not be raised high enough to reach E deck. To compensate for this, the vessel's bow ballast tanks were filled. The bad news was that the ship's natural trim was not restored after loading. The accident happened because the forward doors had not been closed before the ship left dock. With the bow down and the doors open, the sea swept into the vessel and caused it to capsize. This was the deadliest maritime disaster involving a British ship in peacetime since the sinking of HMS *Iolaire* off Stornoway on 1 January 1919, when 205 servicemen returning from the Front were drowned. Only seventy-nine people survived.

At this time, the club rejoiced in having two members called Bill Thomson. One, a farmer from Cessford outside Kelso, was a member from 1983 to 1995. The other, a shipping magnate who ran the Ben Line from Edinburgh, was attending his first dinner. It was he who bet Mr Richard Landale that Russia's policy of *glasnost* would be abandoned by the next dinner. Mr Thomson lost.

Mikhail Gorbachev was general secretary of the Soviet Communist Party from 1985 to 1991, and the final president of the Soviet Union from 1988 to 1991. From the West's perspective, he was a most welcome breath of fresh air. Relatively young (he was born in 1931), vigorous and apparently determined to manhandle his country into the modern world, he attacked corruption in his own country while setting out to negotiate better relations with the West. His reorientation of Soviet strategic aims contributed to the end of the Cold War, ended the political supremacy of the Communist Party of the Soviet Union and led to the dissolution of the Soviet Union. For these efforts, he was awarded the Nobel Peace Prize in 1990. He used language which was seemingly new. *Glasnost* (openness) and *perestroika* (restructuring) had instant appeal to his audience in the West, but were long-established words in the Russian dictionary.

After dinner at Western House, Lowick on 17 April 1988, Mr David Hotham bet Mr Bill Thomson (Cessford) that there would be no women priests in a year's time. Mr Hotham lost.

The ordination of women in the Anglican communion has been the subject of hot debate for many years. Many provinces have accepted it for some time, and an Anglican woman priest was ordained in 1944 in the Diocese of Hong Kong and Macao. But the Church of England resisted it vigorously, with debate lasting from 1975 to 1992, when the General Synod finally approved the ordination of women by a narrow majority of two votes. Mr Hotham lost the vote because the Episcopal Church in Scotland has long-valued women priests.

Mr Frank Usher revealed a spooky foresight when he bet Mr Bill Thomson (Edinburgh) that there would be a major air collision over European airspace before the next dinner.

On Sunday August 28, 1988 in Ramstein, West Germany, near the city of Kaiserslautern, in front of some 300,000 spectators, an aircraft of the Italian Air Force display team collided with other aircraft taking part in a particularly audacious piece of formation flying. Three aircraft crashed to the ground. Sixty-seven spectators and three pilots died, and 346 spectators sustained serious injuries in the resulting explosion and fire.

Several members subsequently focused on the destruction by an arsonist of the Quayside offices of the Tweed Commissioners on Saturday 1 April 1989. All hoped that the culprit would be caught, but suspicion never equalled evidence, so nobody was ever prosecuted for the crime. As a matter of record, the bailiffs employed by the Tweed Commissioners were being notably effective at the time – indeed, they still are – but some of the poachers on the river did not take kindly to the strict regime.

In another event some years later in the Berwick Court, a well-known poacher and petty criminal, who consistently failed to pay his fines, arrived for his hearing with more than £1,000 in cash, realising that if he failed to pay up on this occasion, he would be facing a substantial period in prison. He, for one, enjoyed the sensation of flourishing the money in front of a court public gallery packed with his chums. That night there was a raid on the Court Office in Hyde Hill and the safe was broken open, clearly in an effort to recoup the money. Doubtless the culprit was disappointed that the court staff had wisely banked the cash that day.

The football disaster at Hillsborough, Sheffield, on 15 April 1989 prompted two bets at the dinner two nights later. Even Mr Eric Grounds, who laid the bet, was pleased that his prediction that there would be a similar but smaller disaster somewhere in Europe during the next year was misguided. And Mr Rob Dick optimistically bet Mr Alexander Trotter that England, in spite of Hillsborough and all other problems, would be readmitted to European football. Mr Dick lost.

The incident at Sheffield Wednesday Football Club resulted in the deaths of ninety-six people and 766 being injured, all fans of Liverpool Football Club. It remains the deadliest stadium-related disaster in British history and one of the worst ever international football accidents Moreover, it was the second of two stadium-related disasters involving Liverpool supporters, the other being the Heysel Stadium disaster in 1985.

The match, an FA Cup semi-final tie between Liverpool and Nottingham Forest, was abandoned six minutes into the game. The official inquiry into the disaster, the Taylor Report, concluded that the main reason for the disaster was the failure of police control. The findings of the report resulted in the elimination of standing terraces at all major football stadiums in both England and Scotland.

Four wagers were laid at the 1991 dinner about the Persian Gulf:

- Mr Dick versus Mr Sale, that the Kuwait oil wells would be capped by Christmas 1991. Mr Dick won.
- Mr Grounds versus Mr Trotter that Saddam Hussein would not be in power by the next dinner. Mr Grounds lost.
- Mr Usher versus Mr Sale that Saddam Hussein would still be Iraq's president at next year's dinner. Mr Usher won.
- Mr Sale versus Mr Dick that Saddam Hussein would be assassinated by the next dinner. Mr Sale lost.

Operation Desert Storm (17 January 1991–28 February 1991), commonly referred to as the Gulf War, was a war waged by a United Nations autho-rised coalition force from thirty-four nations led by the USA, against Iraq in response to Iraq's invasion and annexation of Kuwait.

The invasion of Kuwait by Iraqi troops began on 2 August 1990 and was greeted by international condemnation. There were immediate economic sanctions against Iraq by members of the UN Security Council. George H. W. Bush, the US president, deployed American forces into Saudi Arabia, and urged other countries to send their own forces to the scene.

The combat phase was swift and brutal. The Iraq Army was no match for the more sophisticated Alliance forces. But the USA and the United Kingdom were deeply concerned about maintaining good relations within the Alliance, so made the crucial decision not to chase Saddam Hussein's troops the whole way back to Baghdad. Instead they hoped that Hussein would be overthrown by his own people. In the event, he remained in power and a further Gulf War was waged in 2003. Like the first one, it lasted only a few weeks but Saddam Hussein disappeared. It took from

April to December to track him down and arrest him. He was hanged by the Iraqi government on 30 December 2006.

Mr Eric Grounds bet Mr Rob Dick that Terry Waite would not be released before March 1992. In Mr Grounds' opinion Waite was dead. Happily Mr Grounds was wrong.

In 1987 Terry Waite was the Archbishop of Canterbury's assistant for Anglican communion affairs. He had developed a role as an envoy for the Church of England and took part successfully in a number of hostage negotiations in the Middle East. His reputation as an independent was compromised by overt and covert contact with the USA, so when he travelled to Lebanon in January 1987 it was against official advice. He was determined to secure the release of four hostages including the journalist John McCarthy, and believed that he had been promised a safe passage. Almost inevitably (for the time), the hostage takers broke faith and Waite was taken captive on 20 January 1987. He was freed in November 1991 after five years in captivity.

1992 produced some unusual wagers of local and national interest. There were two wagers about the duke of Northumberland. The first was that he would be a bachelor on 1 March 1993, and the second that there would be a khaki duchess of Northumberland (that is, a South American) by the next dinner. Both wagers were lost by Mr Richard Landale.

Hugh Percy, who was a much loved and widely admired man, died in 1988 after forty-eight years as the tenth duke of Northumberland. He was succeeded by his bachelor son, Henry (Harry), who was born in 1953. Harry was unconventional and lived something of a bohemian lifestyle. He played with the notion of film making, which led to gossip about the women in his life. In the event, he died unmarried in 1995 from heart failure after an overdose of amphetamines. His younger brother Ralph succeeded to the title.

Mr Grounds then bet Mr Ian McCreath that there would be a treasure trove find requiring an inquest in North Northumberland before 1 April 1993. Mr Grounds lost.

During the previous summer local treasure hunters at Wooden, outside Kelso, Roxburghshire, found one of the largest seventeenth-century hoards recorded in Scotland. It consisted of 10 gold and 1,365 silver coins, the bulk of them English with a smaller number of Scottish, Irish and Continental issues, which had been deposited about 1643. The discovery was made relatively easy when a plough caught the edge of the box in which the coins were concealed beneath a hedge, dragging a string of coins into the furrow.

Sir David Burnett bet Mr Bill Thomson (Edinburgh) that one of the Maxwell sons of the *Daily Mirror* would be charged in court in connection with the Maxwell empire before 1 April 1993. Sir David won the wager.

Robert Maxwell was born in the small town of Slatinské Doly (now Solotvino, Ukraine) in the easternmost province of pre-Second World War Czechoslovakia. The family were poor, Yiddish-speaking Jews, many of whom died in Auschwitz in 1944. But long before that happened, the man who was then Jan Hoch escaped from his roots and joined the Czechoslovak Army in exile in May 1940.

After the war, Maxwell worked as a newspaper censor for the British military command in Berlin in Allied-occupied Germany. Later, he became the British and US distributor for Springer Verlag, a publisher of scientific books. In 1951 he bought a substantial holding in Butterworth-Springer, a minor publisher. He and his business partner changed the name of the company to Pergamon Press and rapidly built it into a major publishing house.

No stranger to controversy, Maxwell's death on 5 November 1991 was officially described as accidental death by drowning. He was presumed to have fallen overboard from his luxury yacht, the *Lady Ghislaine*, which was cruising off the Canary Islands. But some commentators asserted that it was suicide, while others said it was murder.

His death swiftly exposed the enormous weaknesses in his empire. Banks scrambled to recover their huge loans, and it soon emerged that Maxwell had used hundreds of millions of pounds from his companies' pension funds to shore up the shares of the Mirror Group to save his companies from bankruptcy.

The Maxwell companies filed for bankruptcy protection in 1992. Kevin Maxwell was declared bankrupt with debts of £400 million. In 1995 Kevin and Ian Maxwell and two other former directors went on trial for conspiracy to defraud. They were unanimously acquitted by a twelve-man jury in 1996.

Mr Bill Thomson (Edinburgh) bet Sir David Burnett that there would not be another IRA terrorist explosion of the magnitude of the one which destroyed the Baltic Exchange, the Commercial Union building and the Chamber of Shipping in London the week before. Happily Mr Thomson was right.

On 10 April 1992 the IRA exploded a large bomb in St Mary Axe in the City of London. It was a typical device consisting of fertiliser hidden in a large white truck, and it killed three people, the youngest of whom was fifteen-year-old Danielle Carter. It caused £800 million worth of damage, which some commentators claimed was £200 million more than the total damaged caused by the 10,000-plus explosions that had occurred during the Troubles in Northern Ireland up to that point.

The Baltic Exchange was so badly damaged that it was eventually razed to the ground in 1998, and the site is now graced by the ultra-modern 'Gherkin'.

At the Castle Hotel, Greenlaw on 15 February 1993 there were five wagers about aspects of the war in Yugoslavia. They included challenges that the war would stop, continue or become fiercer, with Sarajevo falling to the Serbs, or the Serbs failing to win a victory. The ideas were as complex as the conflict itself.

Between 1991 and 1995 there was a series of small but entirely vicious wars in the countries of the former Yugoslavia. There was widespread ethnic cleansing. These were the first conflicts since the Second World War to be formally judged genocidal in character, and many key individual participants were subsequently charged with war crimes. Bosnia, Serbia, Croatia and Kosovo all experienced fighting, with Macedonia being the only 'successor' state that experienced no internal conflict.

Sir David Burnett bet Mr Andrew Wailes-Fairbairn that Norman Lamont would not be chancellor of the Exchequer by the time of the next dinner. Sir David was right.

Norman Lamont followed John Major as chancellor of the Exchequer, serving in that role from 1990 to 1993. In part this was his reward for having organised John Major's campaign to become the Conservative Party leader after Margaret Thatcher's resignation. He inherited significant problems, and some commentators, notably Sir Alan Walters, who was Margaret Thatcher's economic adviser, publicly stated that he was the most effective and bravest chancellor since the Second World War.

But politics creates its own tensions, and the relationship between the prime minister and chancellor grew increasingly tense after Black Wednesday, on 16 September 1992, when the Government was forced to withdraw the pound sterling from the European Exchange Rate Mechanism (ERM). Major sought to move Lamont from the Treasury to the Department of the Environment, which Lamont was not prepared to do. He resigned on 27 May 1993. Whatever the reality, his bitterness towards his former colleague and boss was palpable. During his resignation speech in the House of Commons, he said that the government 'gives the impression of being in office but not in power'.

As far back as 1802 a French engineer suggested that a tunnel should be constructed under the English Channel. One hundred and eighty-six years later construction started, with the tunnel opening for passenger business on 14 November 1994. Mr Andrew Joicey, attending his second dinner, bet Mr Bill Thomson (Edinburgh) that the newly opened Channel Tunnel would still be short of rolling stock by the next dinner. Both claimed to have won this wager. In fairness to the operators, they certainly had enough rolling stock to cope with the actual passenger numbers, which amounted to 300,000 in 1994 and 7.3 million in 1995. This compared with a prediction that 15.9 million people would use the tunnel in its first year. Despite the limitation of a slow track network on the English side, volumes rose quickly and 18.4 million used the tunnel in 1998.

Mr Andrew Wailes-Fairbairn bet Mr Richard Landale that Lilburn Estates would be 1,000 acres more than its current 17,500 by 1 January 1996. Mr Landale lost because Langleyford was added to the portfolio.

This is a most helpful bet for providing information about land ownership in the twentieth century. Duncan and Sarah Davidson acquired Lilburn in the 1970s. Thanks to the business success of Persimmon, the house-building business they founded in 1972, the Davidsons steadily accumulated more and more land, creating one of the largest estates in Northumberland, and all of it beautifully maintained. It has proved to be a splendid marriage of commerce and agriculture.

Mr Andrew Douglas-Home bet Mr Bill Thomson (Edinburgh) that the December introduction of catch and release of spring fish would spread to at least one other major river before the next dinner. Mr Douglas-Home lost, but this was the start of a superb conservation strategy which has made the Tweed arguably the finest salmon river in the world.

The practice of catch and release (catching a salmon, unhooking it carefully, and making sure it revives by holding it in the water until it swims away happily) was almost unknown in the United Kingdom, although well practised in the USA, until the mid-1980s. With the reduction in numbers of spring fish (those coming into the river before the end of June) the River Tweed Commission promoted voluntary measures in the mid-1990s. In fact anglers were beginning to return fish alive anyway to save those few spring fish which were caught. This was enshrined in a formal agreement with proprietors in 1998 so that every other fish caught – crucially the first caught – had to be returned and then every other one after that had to be returned alive. This continued on the Tweed until 2010, when the River Tweed Commissioners (RTC) obtained agreement from proprietors that for a period of five years every fish caught up to the end of June had to be returned alive.

At the same time the two main in-river nets (Paxton and Gardo) agreed not to fish for salmon until 15 June; they are compensated for this by the RTC.

Since the early 2000s, it has been illegal to kill a spring (that is up to the end of June) rod caught salmon in the whole of England and Wales, and almost every Scottish river now has voluntary catch and release schemes for its spring fish. The Aberdeenshire Dee, for instance, has for many years had 100 per cent catch and release throughout the whole salmon season, not just for the spring.

It is anticipated that this will continue to be the case until spring salmon stocks recover consistently to the point that returning all salmon alive is no longer considered necessary for conservation reasons. Even then, there has been a huge cultural shift since the 1980s which means that most anglers kill very few salmon and are more than happy to return the majority of what they catch anyway, regardless of any conservation imperatives.

One hundred and forty-seven bets were laid in 1996 and 1997, of which 36 per cent concerned sport of one sort or another and 18 per cent politics. Farming, the IRA, the economy and family celebrations shared the rest of the honours.

1998 introduced two 'new' subjects. The Countryside March on 1 March 1998 was always going to be a big event, with passions running high in rural communities about the government's perceived lack of interest in or understanding of rural affairs. Organised by the Countryside Alliance, members bet that attendance would be anything from 250,000 to 500,000 people. In the event, the BBC judged that 250,000 people marched around a carefully planned route, while the *Independent* said that there were just 142,259 and the organisers claimed 284,500. Scotland Yard said it believed that something in the order of 250,000 people took part. The distinctive characteristic of the march was that it was conducted with great good humour and without a single arrest of any of the participants.

As has often been the case with the wagers laid by members of the club, a simple one-liner tends to conceal a mammoth story. When Mr Rob Dick bet Mr Andrew Joicey that the French police would still be looking for the white Uno by 1 February 1999, the chances are that it would mean nothing to a casual reader in 100 years.

This referred to the car which was alleged to have been involved in the fatal accident which killed Diana, princess of Wales in the early hours of 31 August 1998. Rumour and suspicion were rife. A formal French investigation concluded that the princess's Mercedes, driven by Henri Paul, had come into contact with a white Fiat Uno in the Place d'Alma underpass in Paris before striking the thirteenth pillar supporting the roof of the tunnel at an estimated speed of 65 mph. The driver of that car has never come forward, and the truth is that no one will ever know if it existed. The underlying facts appear to be that Paul had been drinking and he was driving much faster than was prudent for the conditions. It is said that pursuing journalists contributed to his excess speed.

The dinner held at Tillmouth Park Hotel on the night of 15 February 1999 was special because Mr Allan Herriot attended as a guest of the club and received an engraved decanter as a tribute to his long period of membership and his terms of office as secretary and treasurer. By happy coincidence Mr Ronald Barber was chairman for the evening, having lost four bets in 1998, so was able to present the decanter to his father-in-law.

Mr John Burnett, the youngest son of Sir David Burnett, who was a member from 1979 to 1997, was welcomed to his first dinner.

The wagers that night were along traditional lines, but several members enjoyed recording the embarrassment of President Bill Clinton, who was accused of behaving improperly in the Oval Office with Miss Monica Lewinsky, a young White House intern. Lewinsky alleged that she had nine sexual encounters with the president between November 1995 and March 1997. Both parties claimed that they never had sexual intercourse, although they did enjoy a range of activities with Latin names which most ordinary mortals would not be able to translate. The president's problem was that he had developed a reputation for enthusiastic physical activity with a number of women who were not his wife. Clinton was forced to testify before a Grand Jury and narrowly escaped prosecution for perjury.

7
Farming wagers

This section reviews a selection of wagers covering individual crops.

Year	Crop	Proposer	Accepted by
1852	Barley	Hubback Lost	Marshall
1854	Barley	Hubback Lost	Lowrey
1856	Barley	Hubback	Lowrey Lost
1867	Barley	Henderson Lost	Thompson
1871	Barley	Bowhill	Johnson Lost
1874	Barley	Lowrey	Thompson Lost
1879	Barley	Thompson	Lowrey Lost
1886	Barley	Thompson Lost	Lowrey

Sadly Mr Robert Thompson died in 1877 – he was a most helpful contributor to this history.

Year	Crop	Proposer	Accepted by
1890	Barley	Mein Lost	S. Sanderson
1903	Barley	Darling Lost	Carr
1922	Barley	J Darling	Coates Lost
1952	Barley	Maxwell	Davidson Lost

Wager	Result
Price will be 30/- per bale	28/10 ½ to 22/8
Average price will be over 36/- per quarter	32/2
Price will be over 32/- per quarter	46/5
Price will be 5/- lower	1867: 39/1 1868: 41/4
Price will be higher	1871: 29/- to 41/- 1872: 20/- to 44/-
Price will be lower than 36/-	Best 29/- to 30/-
Average price will exceed 25/- per boll	Average was 25/6 Highest 30/- Lowest 21/-
The price will be at least 21/- per boll	Average was 17/6 per boll (23/4 per quarter)
The price will be higher than 21/-	18/- to 20/-
Average price is not better than 1903	1903: 20/- to 21/- 1904: 21/11 to 24/-
Price does not reach 60/-	
That no quarter of Davidson's barley fetches £10	The top price was £7

1954	Barley	Maxwell Lost	Davidson
1962	Barley	Ridley	Davidson Lost
1973	Barley	MacArthur Lost	Wailes-Fairbairn
1981	Barley	De Clermont Lost	Wailes-Fairbairn
1987	Barley	Dick Lost	Thomson (Cessford)
2004	Barley	Crosbie Dawson Lost	Wailes-Fairbairn
2011	Barley	Jeffreys	Pardoe
1845	Wheat	G Henderson Lost	Leitch
1850	Wheat	Hubback Lost	Cockburn
1854	Wheat	G Marshall Lost	Thompson
1860	Wheat	Gilchrist	Innes Lost
1865	Wheat	Henderson	Johnson Lost
1870	Wheat	Hubback	Ruddock Lost
1886	Wheat	Hindmarsh	Bolam Lost
1971	Wheat	Barber	Wailes-Fairbairn Lost
1974	Wheat	MacArthur Lost	Trotter
1981	Wheat	Barber (R)	Trotter Lost
1996	Wheat	Landale Lost	Wailes-Fairbairn
1997	Wheat	Trotter Lost	Wailes-Fairbairn (A)

No field of corn yields over twenty-two bags per acre	Twenty-five acres of BEORNA barley produced twenty-three bags per acre
He won't get 90/- a quarter off the combine	
Price will be between £34 and £36 per ton	Price was £70
Price does not exceed £100 per ton	It was £106–108 and rose to £125
Price will not exceed £120 per ton	It did
Price of feed barley exceeds £110 per tonne	It did not
Price will be below £170 on 1 February 2012	
Price of foreign wheat will not be below 17/-	It was
Price will be at least £1.18.4 per quarter	It was £1.15.6¾
Price will not exceed 60/- per quarter	It was 69/9
Average price will be higher	1860: 43/10 1861: 57/3
Price will be higher by 8/- per quarter on average	Fully 9/- per quarter
Price will be 6/- per boll higher	1870: 29/- 1871: 39/6
Price will not be less than 25/- per boll	It was exactly 25/-
Harvest will not average more than 2 tons per acre	It was 37 cwt
Price will be less than £55 per ton	Average was £63.50
Price will be £105 on the London Futures Market	£105.90
He will average over 4.2 tonnes per acre and get over £125 per tonne	
Price will be in excess of £100	It was £80

2001	Wheat	Dick	Pardoe
			Lost
2006	Wheat	Crosbie Dawson	Joicey
			Lost
2009	Wheat	Jeffreys	Pardoe
		Lost	

No other produce rated as highly as barley and wheat. Over the whole period there have been no more than twenty-one wagers laid about the quality and price of potatoes. Some examples are:

1875   Mr Johnson bet Mr R. Thompson that the price of potatoes will be higher on 5 February 1876 than it was on 5 February 1874. Lost by Mr Thompson. 1874 Reds 70/-, Regents 80/-; 1876 Reds 85/-, Regents 100/-.
1880   Mr Weddell bet Mr Lowrey that red potatoes will not be £4 a ton on 5 February 1881. Lost by Mr Lowrey. The price was only £2.10 to £3.
1884   Mr Robert Thompson bet Mr Lowrey that potatoes will not be less than 80/- per boll on 5 February 1885. Lost by Mr Thompson. The price was 35/- per ton (there are four bolls in a ton).
1974   Mr Barber .bet Lt Col Davidson that potatoes will be £40 per ton by January 1975. Lost by Mr Barber.

Pigs attracted just nine wagers:

1970   Mr Skeggs bet Mr MacArthur that the record for dead pigs at the Royal Show is not exceeded in 1970. Lost by MacArthur. There were no dead pigs, though some were saved from death by the Fire Brigade.
2001   Mr Joicey bet Mr Orpwood that he will have no pigs at all by next year. Won by Mr Joicey.

Sheep were the subject of twelve wagers, of which the most exciting were:

1872   Mr Ruddock bet Andrew Thompson that the sheep on Mr Ruddock's farm will average 20 lb per quarter. Lost by Mr Ruddock.
1903   Mr Carr bet Mr Herriot that Mr Carr, will get a prize for sheep at the Northern Show at Alnwick. Lost by Mr Herriot. Mr Carr received first prize for lambs.

Feed wheat will be £80 or more per tonne	It was £81 in Scotland and £77 in North East England
Price will be above £75	It was £100
Price of feed wheat will be below £110 per tonne	It was £160

2009   Mr Fairfax bet Mr Crosbie Dawson that no Pawston sheep (of any type, sex or breed) will have exceeded the most expensive Mindrum sheep prior to the next dinner. Mindrum lamb made £96 in March 2010. Mr Dawson had no clue, so the secretary's judgement was that he lost.

Cattle also attracted twelve wagers, including:

1883   Mr Logan bet Mr Nicholson that at the forthcoming show of the Northumberland Agricultural Society at Berwick in 1883, the gate money will not be as great as that at the last show at Berwick. In the event that the cattle restrictions are on, the bet to be divided. Lost by Mr Logan. The earlier show raised £438.12.6 and the later one £533.7s.

1935   Captain Goodson bet Captain Carr that Irish cattle are allowed to enter the country free of tax. Lost by Captain Goodson.

1971   Mr Barber bet Mr Wailes-Fairbairn that Mr Wailes-Fairbairn's store cattle in spring 1971 do not average more than £20 over the purchase price. This was lost by Mr Wailes-Fairbairn: the average was £19.8.0.

1972   Mr Sale bet Mr Wailes-Fairbairn that there are more than 39,000 gallons of manure in the pit of his new cattle building on 15 February 1972. This too was lost by Mr Wailes-Fairbairn.

8

Fishing statistics

Every year members bet on the numbers and size of fish caught on the Tweed. Between 1859 and 1890 one wager on the numbers of fish was repeated frequently:

1860   Mr Thompson bet Mr Innes that the gross amount of the produce of the Tweed in season 1860 would be better than in 1859. Lost by Mr Thompson.

	Salmon	Grilse	Trout	Total
1859	8,688	8,987	22,290	39,965
1860	6,724	14,095	18,180	38,999

1873   Mr T. Thompson bet Mr Paulin that the take of salmon, grilse and trout of season 1873 would be lower in the aggregate than that of 1872. Lost by Mr Thompson.

	Salmon	Grilse	Trout	Total
1872	17,245	15,693	22,200	55,198
1873	12,685	18,533	29,531	60,749

1875   Mr Weddell bet Mr Purves that the take of salmon, grilse and trout would be better this season than 1874. Lost by Mr Purves.

	Salmon	Grilse	Trout	Total
1874	9,967	8,725	18,874	37,566
1875	6,414	15,317	16,801	38,532

1876   Mr Smith bet Mr Gilchrist that the take of salmon, grilse and trout would be higher in 1876 than in 1875. Lost by Mr Smith.

	Salmon	Grilse	Trout	Total
1875	6,414	15,317	16,801	38,532
1876	3,788	8,533	11,933	24,254

1879   Mr Smith bet Mr Weddell that the take of salmon, grilse and trout would be better in season 1879 than in 1878. Lost by Mr Weddell.

	Salmon	Grilse	Trout	Total
1878	5,228	2,005	13,627	20,860
1879	3,461	5,083	17,114	25,658

1880   Mr Bolam bet Dr Richardson that the take of salmon, grilse and trout in season 1880 would be greater in number than that of 1879. Lost by Mr Bolam.

	Salmon	Grilse	Trout	Total
1879	3,461	5,083	17,114	25,658
1880	3,052	3,045	8,540	14,637

1882   Mr Paulin bet Dr Richardson that there would be an increase of 5 per cent in the take of salmon, grilse and trout in season 1882 over 1881. Lost by Mr Paulin.

	Salmon	Grilse	Trout	Total
1881	5,195	12,422	17,371	34,988
1882	8,808	3,104	12,399	24,311

In 1890 Mr Paulin bet Mr S. Sanderson that there would be an increase of all kinds of fish (salmon species) landing at the Fish House during the present season compares with the previous one. Lost by Mr Paulin.

	Salmon	Grilse	Trout	Total
1889	4,790	4,468	8,343	17,601
1890	2,466	5,976	19,436	27,878

Price played its part: Mr Paulin bet Mr Sanderson that the price of salmon would be higher per pound in season 1864 than it was in 1863. Lost by Mr Sanderson. 1863, 1/2.3/8; 1864 1/3.3/8.

Mr Paulin bet Mr Sanderson that the average price of salmon of season 1865 would be lower than it was in 1864. Lost by Mr Paulin. 1864 – 1/4. 3/8; 1865, 1/7½ per lb.

Mr Lowrey bet Mr Weddell that the average price of salmon would not be so high in season 1868 as in 1867. Lost by Mr Weddell. 1867, 1/6¾; 1868, 1/4½.

Dr Brown bet Mr Johnson that the price of salmon would be higher on 15 February 1875 than of today (15 February 1874). (2/- per lb). Lost by Dr Brown. 15 February 1874 2/-; 15 February 1875, 1/10.

Dr Richardson bet Mr Paulin the price of salmon would not in season 1881 reach the highest price of season 1880. Lost by Mr Paulin. The highest price in 1880 was 2/9 per lb on 9 March. In 1881 it was 2/6 on 30 March.

Mr Robert Thompson bet Mr Sanderson that the Berwick Salmon Company's shares to be sold that month would not realise ten guineas per share. Lost by Mr Thompson. The price was £11.17.6.

And finally size. It is remarkable how often fish in excess of 40 lb were landed.

Mr Bogue bet Mr Paulin that there would not be a salmon of 40 lb in weight brought into the Fish House during season 1869. Lost by Mr Bogue. One of 48 lb and one of 58 lb were brought in.

Mr Gilchrist bet Mr Robert Weddell that during season 1873 a salmon of 40 lb would be received into the Berwick Salmon Fishery's Company's Fish House. Lost by Mr Weddell. On 15 July 1873 there was one of 45 lb and on 16 July one of 47 lb.

Mr Gilchrist bet Mr Weddell that there would be at least one salmon of 40 lb received into the Fisheries Company's Fish House in 1878. Lost by Mr Weddell. The weights exceeding this were 15 August, 46 lb; 22 August, 41 lb; 26 August, 40 lb, and 16 September, 41 lb.

Mr R. Weddell bet Mr Paulin that there would not be received at the Fish House in season 1880 a salmon exceeding 42 lb. Lost by Mr Weddell, since the top weights were 28 May, one of 44 lb; 23 July, one of 43 lb (and on 17 July one of 40½ lb).

Mr Paulin bet Mr Weddell that there would not be a 45 lb salmon brought into the Fish House in season 1882. Lost by Mr Weddell. The largest was 42½ lb on 24 May, and this was the only fish above 40 lb in the season.

Mr Nicholson bet Mr Willoby that there would not be ten persons charged for salmon poaching before the Norham & Islandshire Justices during the year ended 5 February 1884. Lost by Mr Willoby. There were only seven persons charged.

Mr Paulin bet Mr Weddell that there would not be a 40 lb salmon brought to the Fish House in season 1883. Lost by Mr Paulin. A salmon of 45 lb was brought in on 6 July at Sandsfell.

Mr Weddell bet Mr Paulin that there would not be a 40 lb salmon brought to the Fish House in season 1884. Lost by Mr Weddell. There were six in all.

Mr Weddell bet Mr Paulin that there would be three 40 lb salmon landed at the Fish House in season 1885. Lost by Mr Weddell. Only two were landed. On 14 May there was one of 42 lb and on 2 September one of 40 lb. Note: on 14 September a salmon of 56 lb was got by 'Holmes'.

Mr Paulin bet Mr Weddell that there would be at least three 40 lb salmon landed at the Fish House during season 1886. Lost by Mr Weddell. There were just three fish above 40 lb, the heaviest being 44 lb caught on 31 August at Meadow Haven.

Mr Weddell bet Mr Paulin that there would be at least four 40 lb salmon landed at the Fish House in season 1887. Lost by Mr Weddell. Only three of 40 lb were landed, and they weighed 40, 41 and 42 lb.

Mr Paulin bet Mr Weddell that there would not be more than four 40 lb salmon landed at Berwick Fish House in season 1889. Lost by Mr Paulin. There were seven fish of more than 40 lb.

In 1890 Mr S. Sanderson bet Mr G. Bolam that there would not be a 45 lb salmon landed at the Fish House during the present season. Lost by Mr Sanderson. The heaviest salmon was just 45 lb.

In 1891 Mr Paulin bet Mr Weddell that there would be more than four salmon of 40 lb weight each landed at the Fish House Quay during the present season. Lost by Mr Weddell. There were six weighing, 40, 42, 43, 40, 40, and 45 lb.

In 1893 Mr Weddell bet Mr Paulin that there would be four salmon of 40 lb or upwards landed at the Fish House this season. Lost by Mr Paulin. There were four caught: one of 50½ lb, one of 45, one of 42 and one of 40½ lb.

In 1905 Mr Willoby bet Mr Weddell that there would not be three salmon of 40 lb weight or over landed at the Fish House during the current season. Lost by Mr Willoby. There were three precisely.

In 1913 Colonel Pennyman bet Captain Allenby that no salmon over 42 lb is caught in the Tweed by rod. Lost by Colonel Pennyman. One of 56½ lb was caught by Mr Kidson.

And to add to the mix, in 1921 Captain J. E. Carr bet Mr Caverhill that more herrings would be landed in the harbour than last year. Lost by Carr. It was a very poor season with only 1,712 caught.

In 1922 Colonel Pennyman bet Captain Carr that the Tay produces a bigger salmon than Tweed, to be caught by rod. Lost by Captain Carr. The Tay produced one of 64 lb, the Tweed one of 51½ lb.

9

Oxford and Cambridge competitions

All sorts of competition between Oxford and Cambridge universities was explored between 1904 and 1914, with particularly interesting results in 1911 and 1912.

1904   Rev. Smythe bet Dr C. Fraser that Cambridge would win this year's university boat race. Lost by Dr Fraser. Cambridge won by 4½ lengths.
Captain Norman bet Mr Peters that Cambridge would beat Oxford at this year's cricket match. Lost by Mr Peters. Cambridge won by 40 runs.

1906   Mr Willoby bet Mr Henderson that Cambridge would win this year's boat race. Lost by Mr Henderson. Cambridge won by 3½ lengths.
Mr A. Weddell bet Mr Carr that Oxford would beat Cambridge in the annual sports. Lost by Mr Carr. Oxford won by seven events to Cambridge's three.
Captain Norman bet Captain Orde that Cambridge would win the cricket match at Oxford. Lost by Captain Orde. Cambridge won by 94 runs.

1907   Mr F. Henderson bet Captain Orde that Cambridge win the boat race. Lost by Captain Orde. Cambridge won by several lengths.
Mr Willoby bet Rev. Smythe that Cambridge wins the boat race. Lost by Rev. Smythe.

1908   Mr A. Weddell bet Mr Gregson that Oxford wins the boat race. Lost by Mr Weddell. Cambridge won by 2¼ lengths.
Mr Weddell bet Mr Griffith-Jones that Oxford wins the sports. Lost by Mr Weddell. Cambridge won by six events to four.
Mr Griffith-Jones bet Captain Norman that Oxford would win the cricket against Cambridge. Lost by Captain Norman. Oxford won by two wickets.

Rev. Smythe bet Mr Weddell that Cambridge would win the boat race. Lost by Mr Weddell. Cambridge won by 2¼ lengths.

1910   Mr Gregson bet Mr Carr that Cambridge would win the boat race. Lost by Mr Carr.
Captain Norman bet Mr Askew that Cambridge would win the boat race. Lost by Captain Norman.
Captain Norman bet Mr Askew that Cambridge would win at cricket. Lost by Captain Norman. Oxford won by an innings and 126 runs.
Mr Herriot bet Mr Weddell that a Scotsman would win the King's or St George's at Bisley. Lost by Mr Herriot. The King's was won by Captain Radice of Oxford and the St George's was won by Lt. Humphrey of Cambridge.
Mr Weddell bet Mr Tiffen that Oxford wins the sports. Lost by Mr Weddell. Cambridge won seven to Oxford's three.

1911   Captain Norman bet Mr Askew that Cambridge would beat Oxford at cricket. Lost by Captain Norman. Oxford won by 74 runs. Captain Norman bet Mr Willoby that Cambridge would beat Oxford in the boat race. Lost by Captain Norman. Oxford won in record time by 2¾ lengths. Oxford beat the previous fastest time by over 15 seconds, winning in 18 minutes 29 seconds, a record that would stand for the next twenty-three years. This race was followed by the prince of Wales and his brother Prince Albert, and was the first race in which aeroplanes flew over the competing crews.

1912   Mr Gregson bet Mr Parker that Oxford beats Cambridge in the boat race. Lost by Mr Parker. The race was run twice because of exceptionally stormy conditions which caused both crews to sink on 30 March. Oxford managed to empty their boat and row on to the finish. Pitman the umpire declared the race void and it was rearranged for the following Monday. A gale was still blowing on Monday but with the wind coming from the north conditions were slightly better and Oxford went on to win by six lengths.
Mr Willoby bet Mr Askew that Cambridge will win the cricket match. Lost by Mr Askew. Cambridge won by three wickets.

1913   Captain Allenby bet Mr Askew that Cambridge wins the boat race. Lost by Captain Allenby. Oxford won by ¾ length.
The same two made a bet in relation to rugby, which was lost by Mr Askew. Cambridge won 10–3.
Rev. Smythe bet Mr Willoby that Cambridge wins the boat race. Lost by Rev. Smythe.

1914   Rev. Smythe bet Captain Allenby that Cambridge would win the boat race. Lost by Captain Allenby. Cambridge won by 4½ lengths. Captain Allenby bet Mr Willoby that Cambridge would beat Oxford at cricket. Lost by Captain Allenby. Oxford won by 194 runs.

Biographies

Thomas Allan. See page 7.

Captain Frederick Allenby, CBE, RN. 1864–1934. See page 56.

David Askew (left). A member from 1910–20 but never attended a dinner after 1913. Sheriff of Berwick in 1910 and High Sheriff of Northumberland in 1912.

Henry Askew. Attended just one dinner in 1998. Landowner of the Ladykirk Estate and former vice chairman of the discount brokers, Gerard and National.

Dr Vincent E. Badcock, MC. See pages 65–6.

Anthony Barber. 1909–1988. A member of the club from 1954 to 1982. Brought up at Weetwood and farmed Wrangham, Lowick and Duddo. MFH 1952–68. Chairman of North Northumberland Hunt Fenton Horse Trials. Married Margaret Tweedie 1946. One son.

Ronald Barber, JP (right). Born 3 September 1948, the son of Anthony Barber. Elected to the club in 1980. He

completed four years' service in the Territorial Army (Northumberland Fusiliers). Farmed Duddo, Lowick and Melkington. A JP for twenty-one years and deputy chairman for many years. Married Veronica Herriot 1980 (daughter of Alan Herriot, the longest-serving member). Two sons and one daughter.

Major Ronnie Bell. Elected in 1935 and resigned in 1951, but only attended dinners from 1937 to 1948. Commissioned 1913 into the King's Own Scottish Borderers. Wounded early in the war and taken prisoner, where he remained until 1918. Had three sons who all joined the RAF in the Second World War, but only one, Peter, survived and went to farm in Africa.

James Richardson Black (right), who farmed at Cheswick, was elected in 1891. He attended the dinners in 1892 and 1893 and may well have attended

more: sadly the records between 1894 and 1903 are missing. Nothing more is known about him.

Lieutenant Colonel Sir Francis Blake, Bt, CB, JP (left). Elected at some point between 1894 and 1903. Attended the dinner in 1904 and resigned in 1905. Received baronetcy 1907. MP for Berwick 1916–22. Vice Lord Lieutenant 1920–31.

Sir Michael Blake, Bt (right). Joined the club in 1982 and remains a member as at 2012. High Sheriff of Northumberland 2002. Stockbroker. `Grandson of Lt Col Sir Francis Blake. Married Joan Miller. Two sons.

Thomas Bogue. A member from 1857 to 1869. He lived at Halidon and was mayor of Berwick in 1852, 1858, 1859 and 1864. Sheriff of Berwick in 1854. Died 5 December 1870.

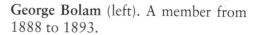

George Bolam (left). A member from 1888 to 1893.

Robert G. Bolam (right). A member from 1879 to 1893.

William Bolam (left). A member from 1904 to 1932. Resigned in 1933.

Dr Alan Bousfield. A member from 1965 to 1981. Educated at Aysgarth and Shrewsbury. Practised as a GP in Wooler.

James Bowhill. A member from 1866 to 1875.

Captain Jack Briggs, MC. See page 57.

Robert Brodie. Attended just one dinner in 1843.

Dr Colville Brown (right). A member from 1869 to 1881. Sheriff of Berwick in 1879.

Major Van Burdon, MC. Lived at Hawkslaw, a mile or two north of Coldstream. A member of the club from 1956 to 1971, when he moved to North Yorkshire. He served in the 11th Hussars during the war.

John Burdon. Attended just one dinner in 1884.

Sir David Burnett, Bt. MBE, TD (opposite top). Born 27 January 1918. A member from 1979 to 1997. Educated at Harrow and St John's College. Cambridge. Served in the Royal Artillery in the Second World War and mentioned in despatches, awarded the MBE and TD. Served in France, North Africa, Sicily and Italy. After the war he was a partner in David Burnett & Sons,

chartered surveyors. He was also on the Board of Hays Wharf (Chairman 1965–80) and was a director of the Port of London Authority and Guardian Royal Exchange. He was master of the Company of Watermen and Lightermen of the River Thames in 1964 and master of the Girdlers Company in 1970. He was a fellow of the Linnean Society and a most gifted watercolour and caricature artist, filling many volumes with pencil sketches of people observed across the dinner or boardroom table. He bought Tillmouth Park Hotel and a certain amount of property in North Northumberland in 1972.

John Burnett (right). Born 29 March 1954. Educated at Harrow and St Edmund Hall, Oxford. A member of the club from 1999 to 2006, John was the third son of David Burnett (the eldest brother, Robert, died at the age of 27). He spent his entire working life as a schoolmaster, first in Sussex and then at Belhaven Hill, a prep school outside Dunbar. He retired to pursue his lifetime interest in walking in the Scottish Highlands, fishing and looking after his house in Sussex.

Sir Ilay Campbell, Bt. A member from 1967 to

1976. Born 29 May 1927, he married Margaret Anderson and had two daughters, Cecilia and Candida. He succeeded to the title in 1967 and was the Scottish agent for Christies from 1968 to 1992.

Lambert Carmichael. A member of the club from 1960 to 1978. He farmed in Scremerston, but had an unusual experience during the Second World War. The North-East produced a secret army of resistance fighters who undertook vital tasks in testing the defences of airfields and army headquarters throughout the invasion 'scare years' of 1940 and 1941. The groups were almost entirely Bedlington miners and formed the Royal Family's personal bodyguard when they were in residence at Balmoral. Their task: to fight off German paratroopers who might have landed with orders to kidnap or even kill the king, queen and the two princesses. Lambert Carmichael was one of these, and regarded the duty as the highlight of his war service. He performed two periods of duty at Balmoral and recalled that the Queen had a good memory. 'She recognised me the second time as "the Tweedside farmer"'. He spoke of grouse shooting with the late king, striding side by side over the hills surrounding Balmoral.

Captain John Evelyn Carr, RN (right). Elected to the club in 1899 but did not attend his first dinner until 1904. He missed very few dinners (1908, 1909, 1933, 1936 and 1938). He resigned in 1939.

Commander Reginald Carr, RN. A member from 1913 to 1927. See page 48.

Dr Thomas Caverhill (opposite top). A member and reliable attender from 1921 to 1933. He only missed the 1932 dinner because of illness, which subsequently led to his resignation in 1934. He was treasurer from 1923 to 1932, handing over to David Herriot.

Digby L. A. Cayley (below). Born
26 September 1864 and died 19 July
1948. A member of the club from 1926
to 1946. Served as a lieutenant in the
Yorkshire Hussars (Yeomanry). DL
for Herefordshire and JP for Lanca-
shire. Three sons, Digby, William and
John.

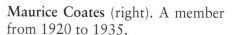

Maurice Coates (right). A member
from 1920 to 1935.

Thomas Cockburn. A member from
1841 to 1861, he was a wine and
spirit merchant in Berwick and died
in 1864.

Dr Collier. A member from 1890
to 1892. Elected in 1889. Died

in 1923. Surgeon lieutenant colonel in the Army Medical Service, having been gazetted first as a staff assistant surgeon from 8 September 1863. Awarded the Abyssinian Medal.

Captain John Carnaby Collingwood (left). An enthusiastic member from 1914 to 1952. See page 70.

Lieutenant Colonel Johnny (Henry Francis) Collingwood, MBE, JP, DL (below). Born 3 May 1905 and died 3 April 1975. He attended his first dinner in 1957 and his final dinner only weeks before he died. Commissioned into the Queen's Bays, he also served with the 4th Hussars and the Somaliland Camel Corps. After the War he conducted business in South America but was called home by his father who saw the need to hand over the estate because of his own health. Sadly Johnny's wife, Nancy Moss, a New Zealander, would neither have children nor live at Cornhill House, so the

marriage foundered. He was dedicated to the community and reluctantly responded to Lord (Matthew) Ridley's exhortation to put himself forward for election to the County Council. To his immense surprise, he was elected. He also served as the sheriff of Berwick when Colonel Jim Smail was mayor and, like his father before him, was chairman of the Berwick Bench.

William N. Crawhall. A member of the club from 1937 to 1946. He served as a captain in the Northumberland Fusiliers, becoming adjutant on 26 June 1939.

Tom Crosbie Dawson (left). Born 1956 and educated at Radley. Became a member of the club in 2001. Married in 1984 Katherine Joicey. Two sons, one daughter. Moved to Pawston, Northumberland in 1990. Enjoys shooting, wine, bird-watching (feathered and other sorts), and is the model bon viveur. Chairman of the College Valley North Northumberland Hunt.

Adam Darling (right). Attended his first dinner in 1895 and his final one in 1921, although he did not resign until 1926. Mayor of Berwick in 1880, 1881 and 1887.

Claude Darling (left). Briefly a member from 1927 to 1930.

James Adam Darling. A member of the club from 1922 to 1931. A grain merchant and director of the family brewing business, Johnson and Darlings, which became Tweed

Brewery & Wine & Spirit Business. That amalgamated with Border Brewery Ltd to become Berwick Breweries Ltd.

Lt Col Horace Davidson, TD, DL (opposite page, with wife Kirsty). Born 1910, died 1982. A member of the club from 1946 to 1981. Served in the KOSB, then farmed Galagate, Norham. Played an active role in local politics (Conservative).

J. D. (Dougal) Davidson. A Northumbrian farmer. A member from 1954 to 1960.

Lt Col Pat De Clermont, DSO. See page 74.

John Dewar. A founder member who was a corn merchant of Bridge Street. He resigned in 1847. He was guardian of the Poor Law Union for Berwick 1849/50.

Robert Dick, FRAgS, FCMI, MA (left). Born 17 July 1939, educated at Harrow School and St John's College, Cambridge. Elected to the club in 1983, he became a long-serving secretary who did a great deal to keep the club going. Married 29 July

1961 Lesley (née Gairdner). Four children, Andrew, Fenella, Michael and David (d. 2010). Farmed at Otterburn, Kelso. Chairman of Agrikem (Borders) Ltd, pesticide distributors of Kelso. Later director of CSC Crop Protection Ltd Perth, and co-founder of Glenteviot Farmers Ltd, a ground-breaking Borders farming cooperative. Tax commissioner. Board Member of the Heather Trust (chairman 2003–07). Chairman of Tricapital Ltd, a Melrose-based business angel umbrella organisation, NXD W Lucy & Co. Ltd, an Oxford-based manufacturer of electrical switchgear, and a number of other companies. Hobbies: good food and wine, tennis, golf, shooting and John Betjeman.

Andrew   Douglas-Home (left). Born 14 May 1950 in Galashiels. Educated at Aysgarth, Eton and Oxford. Elected to the club in 1983. Married 17 May 1980 Jane Pease (b. 21 May 1955). Children Richard, Nicholas and   Freddie   (d.   1990). Qualified as an English CA in 1974, and worked full time in a chartered account-ancy practice until 2003, then as a consultant until 2005. Worked in London, Edinburgh and Kelso. Has lived at the Lees since 1980. A keen and elegant fisher-man, he spent a number of years as chairman of the Tweed Commissioners, having become one in 1982.

John Dunlop. Sadly we have no information about him, other than that he was a member of the club from 1843 to 1860.

Dr Samuel Edgar. See page 7.

Lt Col Tom Fairfax, TD (right). Elected to the club in 1998, Tom Fairfax wears a diverse range of hats in his civilian business life, in which he is responsible for running a   busy   national   consul-tancy practice specialising in cyber security alongside a mixed farming operation at Mindrum. Spent twenty-five years   as   a   reconnaissance soldier   serving   with   9/12 Royal   Lancers   and   the Northumberland   Hussars Squadron   of   the   Queen's

Own Yeomanry. Head of operations with the British Army's principal computer warfare unit, within which he is also an active task leader responsible for leading teams into operational theatres worldwide. He chairs the Crookham Branch of the RBL, was vice chairman of the North Eastern Committee of the Farming Wildlife Advisory Group and supports a range of charities. He runs a modest portfolio of property investment companies. Married to Miki, he has two children, Freddie and Lucia. He plays the ukulele and the Northumbrian bagpipes, and is an enthusiastic amateur watercolourist.

George Farr (left). Born 21 October 1967 in Northampton to a politician/landowner and a Northumbrian Milburn. Became a club member in 2006. Educated at Harrow and Oxford Brooks (nee Polytechnic), then joined the Savoy company as a management trainee, working at the Savoy, Claridges and Connaught Hotels until he met Jane, his wife, and decided that farming and looking after livestock was more rewarding than looking after hotel guests! Moved to Greenknowe near Gordon, Berwickshire in 1993 and completely renovated the house and estate. Later purchased part of Nether Huntlywood and soon after Gordon East Mains. In the interim Pippa, Katkin, Ollie and Jamie were born. In 2005 he sold nearly all of their holdings in Scotland and was repatriated to farm Pallinsburn in England, to which he has since added land at Thrieprigg and part of Castle Heaton. He holds a modest portfolio of property in Newcastle that he rents to students. He has held various voluntary posts within conservation organisations and currently chairs the European Squirrel Initiative. Governor of St Mary's School, Melrose. He is a keen fisherman, cricketer and shot.

Dr Charles Fraser (overleaf). A member of the club from 1889 to 1926. Served in the RAMC during the Great War and was a prisoner of war.

Dr Charles Fraser

His daughter Shena married a Lieutenant Fedden in 1918.

Dr Thomas Fraser (below). A member from 1885 to 1911.

Sir Charles Furness, Bt (left). Born 1900 and educated at Charterhouse and Pembroke College, Cambridge. A member of the club from 1937 to 1955. Married Violet Flower Chipchase Roberts 1930. Three sons, one daughter. Served in the RNVR in the Great War and again as a Lieutenant in the RNVR in 1940–45. Ship owner and landowner. Died 22 June 1974.

Captain Donald Gibsone, RIM, DSO (opposite top). A member from 1925 to 1939. He was gazetted temporary major 21 January 1915 and temporary lieutenant colonel on 28 October 1915. Gazetted 15 June 1915 for distinguished and gallant service but not shown with a DSO in December 1916 when he was deputy director of Inland Water Transport.

Charles Gilchrist (below). A member from 1848 to 1878. He was a grocer in Marygate and elected as a Guardian of the Poor Law Union in 1845. He was mayor of Berwick in 1869.

William H. Gilchrist. A member from 1948 to 1954 but managed to attend only five dinners.

Michael Glover. A member from 1956 to 1959.

Captain Alan Goodson. Born on 1 January 1896. A member of the club from 1932 to 1939. He married Clarisse Adamson on 14 August 1923, lived at Kilham, and died on 11 February 1941.

Delaval Gregson (left). Born 1857, tenth of seventeen children of Henry Knight Gregson of Ford and Eliza Mary Donaldson Selby of Ancroft. Died 29 April 1934. He attended his first dinner in 1908 and remained a member until 1930, although he never attended a dinner after 1928. Resigned in 1930.

Frederick D'Arcy Griffith-Jones (below). Elected in 1908 and resigned in 1921, having attended only one dinner in 1913. He was probably a soldier because his letter of resignation said that he had been posted to Dublin and there was little prospect of him 'again being able to live in that charming n o r t h e r n county'.

Eric Grounds, JP (opposite top with wife Jo). Born in Kansas City, Missouri in 1948, he arrived in England in 1954. Elected to the club in 1987, and on becoming secretary, he c o n v e r t e d the written

records into a digital format on which he based the club history. Educated in England and France, he was commissioned into 1st The Queen's Dragoon Guards in 1966. Served in the Persian Gulf, Aden, Germany, Northern Ireland and Canada. He was adjutant of his regiment in 1976/77 and spent two years working for the Cabinet Office. Mentioned in Despatches 1974. Spent some years as an army and international sportsman in athletics, swimming and bobsleigh, and played rugby for the British Army of the Rhine in 1970/71. Took part in the 1976 Olympic Winter Games in Innsbruck. He was a magistrate on the Berwick Bench from 1989 to 2010 and was bench chairman from 2001 to 2004. High Sheriff of Northumberland 2006/2007. Charity consultant and director 1987 to present. Married Joanna Carey in 1975. One son, two daughters, one of whom is married with a daughter.

Lt Col Philip Harrison, DSO, OBE, JP. Born November 1913, he was commissioned into the King's Own Scottish Borderers. Awarded a DSO in Korea when commanding B Company at the battle known as Guy Fawkes on 4/5 November 1951. He was Sheriff of Berwick in 1963 and died in 1977, having served as KOSB regimental secretary for many years.

Alick Hay. A member of the club from 1980 to 1988. An accountant with a practice in Berwick, he owns Duns Castle. Married with a son and a daughter.

Andrew Henderson. A member of the club from 1842 to 1845.

Frederick Henderson (right). A member of the club from 1904 to 1920.

George Henderson. A member of the club from 1841 to 1859.

George Henderson. A member of the club from 1907 to 1933, although he never attended a dinner after 1928.

Allan Herriot (below). Born 23 August 1920, he was a member of the club from 1948 to 2002. Served in the 7th Gurkha Rifles during the war and returned to the family business, Allan Brothers, where he became the managing director. He was on the Berwick Bench from 1964–90 and was chairman 1985–90. He was sheriff of Berwick in 1968. Died 2009.

David Herriot (opposite page top left). A member of the club from 1885 to 1914. He was sheriff of Berwick in 1897 and mayor in 1899. Died 1919.

David R. Herriot (opposite page top right). A member of the club from 1928 to 1962.

Major James A. Herriot (opposite page below). A member of the club from 1920 to 1946. Served both as sheriff 1932 and mayor of Berwick 1933 and 1934.

Sat on the Berwick Bench. Joint managing director of Allan Brothers with William A. Caverhill from 1919, and became sole MD in 1925 when Caverhill died. He died in December 1946.

James R. A. Herriot. Born 10 October 1952 in Berwick-up-on-Tweed. Elected to the club in 2003. He was educated at Mowden Hall and Fettes College, and attended a finishing school at Ashington Technical College, followed by a brief six-month course at Newcastle Polytechnic to study business. Working career commenced in London as a management trainee in 1971 in retail. Founded Callerton (kitchen furniture manufacturer) 1982 and remains an active director. Married Debbie (Young) in 1978, and produced two children, Louise and Simon. Mad keen salmon fisherman.

William Hindmarsh. A member of the club from 1882 to 1887.

David Hotham. A member of the club from 1980 to 1997. He owned Milne Graden, which he inherited from his mother, but he spent his working life as a correspondent for *The Times* and the *Economist,* which kept him overseas. He was widely recognised as an expert on Turkey in the 1960s and 1970s.

Thomas Hubback. A founder member of the club in 1841 and attended his final dinner in 1872. He was a draper/clothier of Marygate, and guardian of the Poor Law Union for Berwick upon Tweed 1845–51.

W. E. Hume. A member of the club from 1946 to 1948. Sadly we have no other information about him.

James Innes. A member of the club from 1857 to 1860.

Dr William Jamieson (above). A member of the club from 1869 to 1876.

Johnny Jeffreys (opposite top left). Elected to the club in 1996. Born 5 August 1943, he is a farmer of Chillingham Newtown. Married Jennifer Turnbull 1968. One son.

Thomas Johnson (opposite top right). A member of the club from 1862 to 1885.

Hon Andrew Joicey (below). Born 1955. Second son of Michael Edward (Fourth Baron) Joicey and Elisabeth Marion Joicey (née Leslie Melville). Educated Belhaven, Eton and Christchurch, Oxford. BA (Hons) in Agricultural and Forest Science 1977. Married Corinne Cockburn 1994. Three daughters. Director of the New Etal Farming Co. Ltd.

Lord (Michael) Joicey. Born in 1925, he became the 4th Baron Joicey in 1966. He was a member of the club from 1960 to 1992 and was a well-informed and enthusiastic countryman who worked tirelessly for the local community. He died in 1993.

Lt Col George Kennedy, MC. A member of the club from 1950 to 1956. He was

commissioned into the Royal Scots Fusiliers and won his Military Cross during the First World War.

Dr Alexander Kirkwood. A member of the club from 1847 to 1865. He married Mary Prentice Ewing of Edinburgh and had at least one child, Harry, who emigrated to New Zealand and died in Australia.

Richard Landale (above). Born in Northern Ireland in 1943 and educated in Dublin. Elected to the club in 1979. Moved to Northumberland in 1967 and joined Colonel Sale who was the senior partner of John Sale & Partners; became a partner in 1972. A tax commissioner for many years and chairman from 2000–05. Became secretary of Kelso Races Ltd under the chairmanship of Reg Tweedie in 1985 and MD from 1995. Married Jennifer Jeffreys in 1971. Three sons. A keen sportsman, especially fishing, and a particularly highly regarded bon viveur.

Colonel Gerald Leather (opposite page). Attended just one dinner in 1931. He inherited the Middleton Estate from his father, Frederick Leather, who had little interest in the substantial property bought by his father, John, in 1857. The Middleton Hall website says 'On John's death in 1885, Frederick abandoned the buildings to a slow decline, choosing instead to waste his family fortune on his numerous vices.' It seems that Gerald Leather tried hard to restore some of his family's inheritance but had a 'maverick' approach which led ultimately to the property being sold piecemeal.

Lt Col Mark Leather, MC. Born 1910. A member of the club from 1964 to 1966. Educated at Wellington College and Sandhurst, and commissioned into the Durham Light Infantry (DLI) in 1930. In 1937 he joined the Sudan Defence Force and fought in Abyssinia against the Italians in 1940–41. Rejoined 1st Battalion DLI in September 1943 on the island of Cos, days before they were overwhelmed by the Germans. He was badly wounded by a mortar on 3 October 1943 and was taken prisoner while receiving treatment in hospital.

He was in several POW camps until being sent to Oflag 79 near Brunswick, which was not liberated until 11 April 1945. He was awarded the MC for his contribution on Cos and was promoted to Lt Col after the war to command 2 DLI from 1952 to 1955.

Neil Leitch. A member of the club from 1843 to 1848.

Captain Christopher Leyland. Attended just one dinner in 1927. His grandson offered an amusing insight to his life: see page 46. He died in 1970.

Commander Hugh Lillingston, RN (right). Born 16 August

1878 and died 23 September 1952. A member of the club from 1930 to 1939. In 1908 he was a lieutenant on HMS *Victorious* where his captain was Henry H. Torlesse. He married Amy Margaret Milne Home, daughter of David Milne Home of Wedderburn and Paxton. One son, George David, born 1923.

John Lindsay. A farmer of Cornhill on Tweed, attended just two dinners in 1948 and 1949.

Frederick Logan. A member of the club in 1866 and 1867.

John Logan (above). A member of the club from 1880 to 1886.

Ross Logan. A member of the club from 1959 to 1968.

William Logan. A member of the club from 1848 to 1862.

John Lovett (left). Elected to the club in 1995. After working in London moved to Hetton House in 1989. Married to Jane; one son and two daughters. Chartered accountant (ICAS) and company director. Fishery proprietor – Lower North Wark (Tweed) and Hetton House (Till). River Tweed Commission – Council member since 1990, member of Management Committee 1994–2005, chairman of Council 1998–2004. Tweed Foundation trustee 1992–2005, chairman of Board of Trustees 1998–2004. Atlantic Salmon Trust member of Council of Members since 1999. Tweed

Rivers Fisheries Association chairman since 2004.

Alexander Lowrey. See page 11. A founder member of the club in 1841, he remained a member until he died in 1889. Farmer of Castle Hills. Elected to be a guardian of the Poor Law Union March 1845.

Michael Lyndon Skeggs (left). Born 10 June 1926. A member of the club from 1964 to 1986. Educated at Maidwell Hall and Uppingham, he took the university short course at Oxford and was then commissioned into the Royal Marines. He served at the Royal Navy Headquarters in Hamburg. After leaving the Marines, he spent four years in Nigeria with John Holt (Liverpool) Ltd, engaged in shipping and trade. On his return to the United Kingdom in 1952, he trained as a land agent on the Cawdor Estate in Wales.

There he met and married Barbara Evans, nee Rogers. Joined Strutt & Parker in Wales and moved to Chelmsford in Essex. In 1960 he joined John Sale in Northumberland and became a partner. After his retirement in 1986 he took to making rocking horses and built 129, while mending many others. Two daughters.

Archie MacArthur (right). The only person in the club's history to have been elected twice. He attended his first dinner in 1954 but never attended a second dinner and resigned in 1956. During 1964 he intimated to a friend that

he would welcome an invitation to rejoin, so he was duly elected and attended the dinner in 1965. His final dinner was in 1982. He was a farmer at Tiptoe outside Cornhill on Tweed.

David MacBeath. Elected to the club in 1862 and attended just one dinner in 1864.

William MacDonald (left). A member of the club from 1879 to 1881.

Lt Col Lionel Machin, MC. Born 17 August 1893. A member of the club from 1951 to 1964. Commissioned 17 February 1915. Commanded the 7th (Galloway) Battalion KOSB 1940–42. He married Constance Marion Gough in 1923 then married Lois Edith Barstow in 1968. Mentioned in Despatches 1917. MC awarded at the third battle of Ypres. Retired 28 March 1947. Died 3 April 1974.

Dr Philip Maclagan, OBE, MC. A member of the club from 1931 to 1955. Medical officer with Royal Northumberland Fusiliers during the Great War. Sheriff of Berwick 1930.

Neil Maconachie. A member of the club from 1976 to 1980 and seems to have been one of the very few members who was asked to resign after sliding beneath the table unconscious. See page 91.

Andrew Mallock. A member of the club from 1847 to 1855. He died on 26 March 1855.

D. M. Marshall. A member of the club from 1954 to 1963.

George Marshall. A member of the club from 1841 to 1857.

James Marshall. A member of the club from 1848 to 1860. He was a grocer in Bridge Street and was elected to be a guardian of the Poor Law Union in March 1845.

Major Eustace Maxwell. Born 24 February 1913, died playing tennis on 12 April 1971. A member of the club from 1951 to 1957. Married Dorothy Vivien Belville. Children Diana Mary Maxwell, born 1942 and Sir Michael E. G. Maxwell, Bt, born 1943.

(Henry) Crichton McCreath. A member of the club from 1936 to 1951. The third son of Henry Gourlay McCreath, he served as a captain in Ladykirk (H) Company, KOSB Volunteers. A solicitor, and until his retirement a partner with what was then Dickinson Miller & Turnbull (now Dickinson Dees) in Newcastle. Married with one daughter, Ann.

Ian McCreath, MBE. Born 24 November 1944, the son of William 'Bill' McCreath. A member of the club from 1984 to 1994. Admitted as a solicitor in July 1967 and appointed as coroner for North Northumberland from 3 December 1979. He retired in 2008. He served as a governor of Longridge Towers School from 1982 to 2011 and with distinction as chairman of the governors from 2000 to 2011.

William 'Bill' McCreath. Born on 18 February 1919 and died on 16 February 2007. A member of the club from 1953 to 1986. While still a schoolboy, his left leg was amputated, but he was able to lead a long and fulfilling life. He practised as a solicitor in Berwick-upon-Tweed/North Northumberland from 1948 to 1984. He was president of Berwick Rotary Club in 1968/69, president of Berwick St Andrews Club in 1970, first chairman of Berwick Parish Church Trust, and captain of Berwick-upon-Tweed (Goswick) Golf Club in 1953.

Kenneth McKenzie. Attended the first meeting of the club in 1841 and was never heard of again.

Ian McKie (right). Became a member of the club in 2008.

Lived and farmed at Twyford in Buckingham from 1985. Enjoyed a successful amateur racing career before hunting the Bicester Hounds from 1987 and then the College Valley North Northumberland Hounds from 2003. Moved to Lanton in 2003 with his wife Victoria and two daughters Jessica and Rosie. Lanton is a mixed farm of arable and livestock but his main farming interest is to develop and promote the Lanton herd of Luing cattle. Enjoys all country sports and takes particular pleasure from running a small shoot and searching for a sea trout on the Glen.

John Meggison. A member of the club from 1857 to 1865. He had previously been a member of the Tweed Salmon Club in 1855–56. Accountant. Sheriff of Berwick 1860. Died 5 February 1866.

James Mein (left). A member of the club from 1890 to 1903. Although we know nothing about him, other than he lived at Lamberton, it is possible that he played rugby for Scotland against England in 1871.

William Miller. A member of the club from 1868 to 1870.

James Nicholson. A member of the club from 1882 to 1885. He died in 1887.

Captain Francis Norman, RN (see page 36). A member of the club from 1882 to 1910 and was consistently unsuccessful with his wagers, losing eighty-eight and winning fewer than ten. He joined the Navy at the age of 14 serving first on HMS *Havannah*. Later he was on *Britannia* and served in the Crimea, landing at Balaclava and fighting at Inkerman. He arrived in Berwick from Bexhill in Kent in 1877 and lived at Cheviot House. Sheriff of Berwick 1884 and 1866. Mayor 1888 and 1890 He was a member of the Scottish Alpine Botanical Club and an enthusiastic participant in the affairs of Berwick Naturalists. He ran the fundraising for the Flodden memorial and paid for and erected the Diamond Jubilee fountain for Queen Victoria. He was the author of the *Official Guide to the*

Fortifications of Berwick published in 1907. There is a memorial to him in the town. He died in October 1918.

Captain Henry Orde, JP (left). Born 4 November 1838, he was elected to the club in 1906 but attended only one dinner in 1907, resigning because he intended to leave the area. He became a captain in the 15th Regiment, East Yorkshire. Married in 1861, Rosa Anne Repp from Copenhagen. Children Leonard, Thorleif, Roden and Rosa Emily. He was one of the many subscribers to the *History of Northumberland* published in 1897.

Simon Orpwood (right). Elected to the club in 1999. Joint Master of the College Valley North Northumberland Foxhounds from 1992 to 2008. Fellow of the Royal Agricultural Societies of Great Britain (FRAgS). Vice president of the Royal Smithfield Club and a governor of the Commonwealth Agricultural Society. Married Caroline Mayne 1982. Three sons.

Edward Osborne. Attended just one dinner in 1920.

Lord Francis Osborne (right). Born 11 March 1864, died 17 October 1924. Son of the 9th Duke of Leeds. Married 1896 Blanche Ruth Brooke Tatton Grieve (1869–1956) Served in the Royal Navy. A member of the club from 1920 to 1923.

Terence Pardoe (below). Born 1946. Elected to the club in 2001. Educated at Terrington Prep school, Haileybury and ISC whence he gained entry to Edinburgh University to attend the Edinburgh and East of Scotland Agricultural College. Chief executive of Coastal Grains Ltd, having set it up in 1982. Married with two children,

one of whom is married with two boys.

Henry Parker (opposite top). Became a member between 1893 and 1904 but never attended dinner until 1910. He resigned after the 1912 dinner.

George Paterson. Attended the first dinner in 1841 and was never seen again.

Alastair Paton. A member of the club from 1936 to

1964. He was a tall man (6ft 10 in) and trained horses with mixed success. He lived for some time at Tindall House near Etal.

George L. Paulin (below left). Elected a member of the club in 1861 after the death of his father, William. He took part from 1862 to 1893. He was an accountant and lived at Leeside, Berwick. He was elected a Fellow of the Huguenot Society in 1892.

William Paulin (below right). A member of the club from 1847 to 1861, although he last attended a dinner in 1858.

Colonel Alfred Pennyman (see page 49). Born 1858. A member of the club from 1912 to 1934. The family came from Ormesby Hall, Yorkshire. He was commissioned in 1878 and served in the 25th Regiment KOSB. Lived at Ord Cottage. Great horseman and steeplechaser.

Henry Peters (left). A member of the club from 1882 to 1907. Sheriff of Berwick 1890. Died 20 May 1907.

James Purves. A member of the club from 1869 to 1877. Mayor of Berwick 1866, 1872 and 1874. He may also have been a member of the Tweed Salmon Club.

Dr Henry Richardson. A member of the club from 1865 to 1885. Sheriff of Berwick in 1865. Died October 1885.

Henry Richardson (right). Elected some time between 1894 and 1903 so our records only show his attendance at the 1904 dinner.

John Ridley. A member of the club between 1952 and 1971.

Major John 'Jock' Robertson. Born in Hong Kong in 1902, the only son of Harry Robertson, Taipan for Butterfield and Swire, and Lilla Macfarlan. A member of the club from 1946 to 1979. Educated at Sedbergh and Oxford before returning to China to join his father's company and the Shanghai Light Horse, part of the volunteer corps for the international settlement. He met Helen Milne Home of Paxton when she visited Hong Kong, they were married in London in 1933, and later he took the surname Home Robertson. On his arrival in Berwickshire, he joined the 4th (territorial) Battalion of the KOSB and served through the 1939–45 war. He was adjutant for the Battalion during the brief and perilous excursion from Cherbourg to Le Mans and back in June 1940 in the second British Expeditionary Force to France (after Dunkirk). He continued to play an active part in the work of the TA for many years. He was a Deputy Lieu-tenant for Berwickshire, a Justice of the Peace, a prominent Roman Catholic, and a very enthusiastic gardener.

Joseph Ruddock. A member of the club from 1867 to 1872. Mayor of Berwick 1865. Died 27 December 1874.

Lieutenant Colonel John Sale, OBE. A member of the club from 1934 to 1939.

Tom Sale, OBE (right). Born 1933, died 2011. A member of the club from 1972 to 1997. Attended the Royal Agricultural College, Cirencester where he was awarded the Harker Silver Medal in 1957. Land agent and partner with Sale & Partners. Served as a TA officer in the Royal Northumberland Fusiliers. High Sheriff of North-umberland 1985. Married Margot Middleton. Two sons.

Evan Sanderson (right). A member of the club from 1886 to 1893. He was sheriff of Berwick in 1889 when Captain Francis Norman was mayor.

George Sanderson. Attended the first two dinners in 1841 and 1842. Nothing more is known about him.

Stephen Sanderson (below). A member of the club from 1857 to 1892. Sheriff of Berwick 1865.

Andrew Scott. Attended the first five dinners of the club between 1841 and 1845.

Henry Short. Attended the first four

dinners of the club between 1841 and 1844.

W. R. Sitwell. Attended two dinners in 1952 and 1953.

George Smith. Attended one dinner in 1868 and died in January 1869.

John Smith (right). A member of the club from 1875 to 1879.

Captain William Smith, RN (left). Attended one dinner in 1862. Lived at Ava Lodge. He was sheriff of Berwick in 1845 and mayor in 1849.

Rev. W. M. Smythe (below left). Said to have been elected to the club in 1900. He resigned in 1925, having attended ten dinners.

Mr Stevenson (first name unknown). Attended one dinner in 1847.

James Stevenson (below right). A member of the club from 1893 to 1905 but only attended three dinners in 1893, 1904 and 1905.

Surgeon Commander John Stoddart. Attended one dinner in 1933.

Andrew Thompson

W. J. (Billy) Straker Smith. A member from 1971 to 1973. See page 85.

Percy Swan. A member of the club from 1933 to 1937 but did not resign until 1950.

Andrew Thompson (left). A member of the club from 1864 to 1884. Mayor of Berwick 1863, 1867, 1870, 1875 and 1876; sheriff in 1877. Died 1884.

Robert Thompson. A member of the club from 1873 to 1887, the year in which he died.

Thomas Thompson (right). A member of the club from 1844 to 1878. He resigned in February 1879 and died 21 January 1880.

John Thomson. A member of the club from 1843 to 1846.

Bill Thomson (opposite top). A farmer of Cessford, a

Bill Thomson

member of the club from 1983 to 1995. He has been on the board of eight farming and related businesses and is currently chairman of WCF Ltd, with whom he has been a director for thirty years. Past president of the Borders Area of the National Farmers Union and long-serving elder of Morebattle church.

Bill Thomson. A shipping magnate and Chairman of Ben Line, Edinburgh, a member of the club from 1987 to 1997.

Robert Thorp. Attended just one dinner in 1946.

Joseph Tiffen (right). A member of the club from 1897 to 1934 and served as treasurer from 1907 to 1923.

Alexander Trotter (overleaf). Born 20 February 1939. Son of Major H. R. Trotter and Rona née Murray. Elected to the club in 1973. He has lived at Charterhall since 1946. Educated at Ludgrove and Eton. Commissioned into the Royal Scots Greys 1958 and served in BAOR three times plus a bit of Aden, Hong Kong, Libya and a band tour for three months in USA and Canada as admin officer. Last military appointment was as a helicopter pilot and

officer commanding s reconnaissance squadron. Studied business management at City of London Tec and worked in the city for a year before returning to run Charterhall. Also worked in the building industry in Ryedale Construction till 1972. Married Julia Greenwell from Suffolk in 1970. Three sons, Henry, Edward and Rupert. Started Meadowhead Ltd (caravan park developers and managers) in 1973. Worked with Scottish Landowners Federation as committee chairman, convener and president, then chairman of Nature Conservancy Scotland (a forerunner of Scottish Natural Heritage). Lord Lieutenant of Berwickshire 2000 to present. Sports: speed and field, raced cars, horses and on skis plus field sports. MFH Berwickshire 1981 to 1991 then chairman.

Johnny Trotter (right). Born 12 May 1948, the younger brother of Alexander, a member of the club from 1989 to 1994. Served as an officer in the Royal Scots Greys and the later amalgamated regiment, the Royal Scots Dragoon Guards (Carabiniers and Greys) from 1968 to 1973. He left the army to become a director of Dobbies Garden Centres and the owner of Mortonhall Garden Centre (1975–86). Continues to be a freelance garden designer. Other interests include fishing, sailing and shooting. Married Julia Crombie in 1974.

Frank Usher. A member of the club from 1983 to 1997. The owner of a large estate, he briefly represented Great Britain as a bobsleigher in the late 1960s in company with other notable lowland Scots like Tony Fildes and James Manclark.

Andrew Wailes-Fairbairn. A member of the club from 1964 to 2004. He farmed at Berrington and served for many years as a tax commissioner.

Rupert Wailes-Fairbairn (left). The son of Andrew, elected to the club in 1995. He farms Berrington and is also an insurance expert with Lycetts.

Blake Weatherhead (left). A member of the club from 1888 to 1893.

Major John Weatherhead (over leaf). A member of the club from 1880 to 1913. He was sheriff of Berwick in 1885 and died 23 February 1914.

Arthur Weddell. A member of the club from 1906 to 1920. He was club secretary from 1909 to 1922. See page 16.

James C. Weddell. A member of the club from 1841 to 1882. He died in 1883. See page 16.

Robert Weddell, VD Born 23 November 1843. A member of the club from 1869 to 1908. Solicitor. Had 40 years service in the 1st Volunteer Battalion Northumberland Fusiliers, retiring as a colonel. He married Mary Short of Bamburgh. One son and one daughter. Died 26 January 1909. See page 16.

Edward Willoby. See page 6.

Edward Willoby Jr (below). A member of the club from 1886 to 1920. He worked as a land agent.

Major John Weatherhead

Caricatures of members by Sir David Burnett

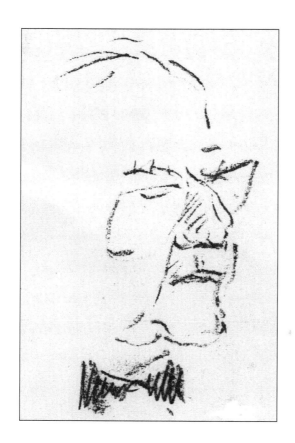

Anthony Barber

Ronald Barber

Sir Michael Blake

Sir David Burnett (by Colin Smith)

Lt Col Pat de Clermont

Horace Davidson

Robert Dick

Andrew Douglas-Home

Eric Grounds

Allan Herriot

David Hotham

Hon. Andrew Joicey

Lord (Michael) Joicey

Richard Landale

Michael Lyndon Skeggs

Archie MacArthur

Ian McCreath

Bill McCreath

Tom Sale

Bill Thomson (of Cessford)

Alexander Trotter

Johnny Trotter

Frank Usher

Andrew Wailes-Fairbairn

General index

Index of members